DK EYEWITNESS TOP 10 TRAVEL GUIDES

MIAMI

AND THE KEYS

JEFFREY KENNEDY

DK PUBLISHING

Left **Deco District** Right **Domino players, Little Havana**

LONDON, NEW YORK, MUNICH,
MELBOURNE, AND DELHI

Produced by Blue Island Publishing
Reproduced by Colourscan, Singapore
Printed and bound in Italy by Graphicom

First American Edition, 2003
03 04 05 06 10 9 8 7 6 5 2 3 1

Published in the United States by DK Publishing,
Inc., 375 Hudson Street, New York, New York 10014

A Catalogue of Publication record is
available from the Library of Congress

ISBN 0-7894-9185-0

Within each Top 10 list in this book, no hierarchy
of quality or popularity is implied. All 10 are, in the
editor's opinion, of roughly equal merit.

Floors are referred to throughout in
accordance with American usage;
i.e., the "first floor" is at ground level.

See our complete product line at
www.dk.com

Contents

Miami's Top 10

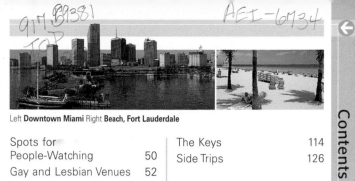

Left **Downtown Miami** Right **Beach, Fort Lauderdale**

Left **Alley off Worth Avenue, Palm Beach** Right **Biltmore Hotel, Coral Gables**

Key to abbreviations
Adm *admission charge payable* **Free** *no admission charge*

MIAMI'S
TOP 10

MIAMI'S TOP 10

ᵀᴼᴾ10 Highlights of Miami

At its best, Miami is all pastel hues and warm, velvety zephyrs – a tropical reverie. The culture is sensuous and physical, often spiked with Caribbean rhythms and accents. Outdoor activities hold sway throughout the area, at the world-famous beaches and in the turquoise waters; the vibrant nightlife, too, attracts pleasure-seekers, while significant historical sights are around every corner.

1 SoBe Life
Ever since *Miami Vice* (see p72) drew attention to this fun-zone, hedonists have flocked for the beaches and nightlife (see pp8–9).

2 Deco District
The whimsical architecture on South Beach ultimately traces its roots back to 1920s Paris (see p13), but it underwent fruitful, exotic influences along the way and blossomed into Florida's own Tropical Deco (see pp10–13).

3 Calle Ocho, Little Havana
The Cubanization of Miami changed it from sleepy resort to dynamic megalopolis. Little Havana fuels the impression that Miami is Latin American at heart (see pp14–15).

4 Villa Vizcaya
One immensely rich man's aspiration to European grandeur and appreciation of Western artistic heritage led to the creation of what is probably Miami's most beautiful cultural treasure (see pp16–17).

5 Merrick's Coral Gables Fantasies
The 1920s boom saw a need to build not only structures but also an identity. George Merrick rose to the challenge and created fantasy wonderlands that continue to stir the imagination today (see pp18–19).

Previous pages **Marlin Hotel, South Beach**

Lowe Art Museum
6 This major art museum, created by an endowment from George Merrick, has around 12,000 works of art, including masterpieces from cultures the world over, and from every age *(see pp20–21).*

The Wolfsonian 7
This superb museum (which began life as a storage company) owes much to its founder's passion for collecting 20th-century propaganda art and design artifacts of the period 1885–1945 *(see pp22–3).*

Gold Coast Highway A1A
8 Route A1A hugs the sands of the Gold Coast, wending through Florida's wealthiest and most beautiful areas *(see pp24–5).*

Key West 9
This mythic isle lives up to its reputation as the most outlandishly free spot in the US. A frothy mix of maritime traditions and laid-back style *(see pp26–7).*

The Everglades
10 Taking up most of South Florida, the Everglades is a vast sea of swamp and sawgrass, dotted with subtropical forests and populated with prolific wildlife. It is also home to Native American Seminoles and Miccosukees *(see pp28–9 & p41).*

SoBe Life

The nickname for Miami's beautiful South Beach was inspired by Manhattan's SoHo, and it's become every bit as fashionable and hip as its New York counterpart. Now the "American Riviera" is an ebullient mix of beach life, club-crawling, lounge-lizarding, and alternative chic, attracting devotees from around the globe. Yet, SoBe's modern posh character is also nicely blended with just the right amount of tacky kitsch and downright sleaze.

1 Ocean Drive

Strolling, skating, or biking along this beachfront strip is the way the locals do it. From about 6th Street and north, take in the toned, tanned athletes, the abundant, ice-cream-colored Art Deco architecture *(see pp10–13)*, and the people-watching cafés.

News Café

🚗 Parking is a problem everywhere along here, so once you find a place, leave the car and walk. Be aware that you'll need to feed the meter a feast of coins, unless you choose one of the parking garages.

🅿 To participate fully in the SoBe experience, the News Café should definitely be your choice for eats.

Map R–S 3–6

Top 10 Attractions

1 Ocean Drive
2 Lummus Park Beach
3 News Café
4 Casa Casuarina
5 Marlin Hotel Bar
6 Collins and Washington Avenues
7 Old City Hall
8 Española Way
9 Lincoln Road Mall
10 SoBe Clubs

2 Lummus Park Beach

This swath of busy park and 300-ft (90-m) wide beach *(below)* stretches for ten blocks, from 5th St north. Much of the immaculate sand was imported.

3 News Café

The café-restaurant at 800 Ocean Drive continues to be action central for SoBe social life. Sit and read the morning paper, available in several languages, over a full breakfast – or just watch the action.

Beach Patrol Headquarters

4 Casa Casuarina

1114 Ocean Drive (not open to the public) was bought by fashion designer Gianni Versace in 1993 for $3.7 million. He was gunned down on its steps in 1997. The Mediterranean-Revival style building was formerly called Amsterdam Palace.

5 Marlin Hotel Bar

The sparkling hotel at 1200 Collins Avenue *(right)* sports one of SoBe's best places to while away the time with locals. The décor is the apotheosis of the chrome aesthetic – everything seems to be made of curving aluminum.

For the Deco District **See pp10–13**

6 Collins and Washington Avenues

These scruffier, funkier cousins of Ocean Drive offer kinky shops and top nightclubs, but also some fine Art Deco buildings of their own, including the Miami Beach Post Office.

7 Old City Hall

The 1920s Mediterranean-Revival, buff-colored tower *(left)* is a distinctive South Beach landmark. Its red-tile roof can be seen for blocks around. The building is now a courthouse.

8 Española Way

Between 14th and 15th streets, and Washington and Drexel avenues, Española Way is a Mediterranean-Revival enclave that is all salmon-colored stucco, stripy awnings, and red-tile roofs. It now houses boutiques and offbeat art galleries. Built in 1922–5, it was meant to be an artists' colony but instead became an infamous red-light district at one stage of its history.

Gay Renaissance

South Beach is now world famous as a top gay vacation destination. It is estimated that up to half of the Deco District apartments are gay-occupied. Rainbow flags are everywhere you look, indicating gay-friendly businesses. Gay festivals attract thousands from around the world, flocking to the all-night raves and beach parties. A culture of the Body Beautiful thrives here, which, combined with the constant ebb and flow of revelers, makes the area a vast playground for the sexually various. Gay people now enjoy considerable political clout, both locally and statewide.

9 Lincoln Road Mall

Built in the 1920s as an upscale shopping district, it became one of the country's first pedestrian malls in the '60s. Its current incarnation with art studios and galleries is the brainchild of the South Florida Art Center.

10 SoBe Clubs

Most of South Beach's top clubs are located on Washington and Collins avenues, between 5th and 16th streets. Few get going until at least midnight. Choose between straight, gay and mixed venues *(see pp76–7)*.

For more on SoBe's nightlife **See pp58–9**

Deco District

SoBe's Art Deco District consists of some 800 preserved buildings, the cream of them along Ocean Drive. This splendid array of structures embodies Miami's unique interpretation of the Art Deco style, which took the world by storm in the 1920s and '30s. Florida's take on it is often called Tropical Deco (see pp12–13), which befits the fun-and-sun approach to life. Often hotels were made to look like ocean liners (Nautical Moderne) or given the iconography of speed (Streamline Moderne).

Park Central

🕐 Guided tours are offered on Saturdays and Thursdays. Otherwise, a self-guided audio tour can be rented from the Art Deco Welcome Center.

🍴 Mango's Tropical Café, at 980 Ocean Drive, lives up to everything its name might imply – florid and steamy, and always very happening.

Map R–S 3–4
• Miami Design Preservation League and Art Deco Welcome Center, 1001 Ocean Drive at 10th, in the Oceanfront Auditorium
• 11am–4pm daily

Top 10 Buildings

1. Park Central
2. Beacon Hotel
3. Colony Hotel
4. Waldorf Towers
5. Breakwater Hotel
6. Beach Patrol Stations
7. Clevelander Hotel
8. Leslie Hotel
9. Cardozo Hotel
10. Cavalier Hotel

Park Central
A 1937 favorite by Henry Hohauser, the most famous architect in Miami at the time. Here he used the nautical theme to great effect.

Beacon Hotel
The abstract decoration above the ground floor of the Beacon has been brightened by a contemporary color scheme, an example of "Deco Dazzle," introduced by designer Leonard Horowitz in the 1980s.

Colony Hotel
Perhaps the most famous of the Deco hotels along here, primarily because its stunning blue neon sign *(left)* has featured in so many movies and TV series.

Waldorf Towers
Here is one of the first examples (1937) of Nautical Moderne, where the style is carried to one of its logical extremes with the famous ornamental lighthouse on the hotel's roof. Fantasy towers were the stock in trade for Deco architects.

5 Breakwater Hotel
The classic Streamline Moderne hotel *(left)* was built in 1939. It features blue and white "racing stripes," which give the impression of speed, and a striking central tower that recalls both a ship's funnel and Native-American totems.

6 Beach Patrol Stations
Even the lifeguard stations are done up in Deco on South Beach. Looking perhaps more like a homemade flying saucer that has just landed on the beach, these pink and yellow follies embody the spirit of fun that pervades the lifestyle.

South Beach (SoBe)

15TH STREET

11TH STREET

9TH STREET

7TH STREET

7 Clevelander Hotel

Albert Anis used classic Deco materials – especially the glass blocks in the hotel's bar, which is now a top South Beach neon-lit nightspot. Typical Deco features include vertical fluting, geometric decorative touches, the "eyebrow" overhangs shading the windows, and the stripy lettering on the sign.

8 Leslie Hotel
The Leslie (1937) is cockatoo-colored, white and yellow with gray accents *(below)* – a color scheme typical of those currently in favor along Ocean Drive. Originally, however, Deco coloring was quite plain, usually white with only the trim in colors. Nor were the backs of the buildings painted, since money was too tight in the 1930s to allow anything more than a jazzy façade. The Leslie's interior has recently been renovated.

9 Cardozo Hotel
A late Hohauser work (1939) and the favorite of Barbara Capitman *(see p13)*, this is a Streamline masterpiece, in which the detail of traditional Art Deco is replaced with beautifully rounded sides, aerodynamic racing stripes, and other expressions of the modern age. The terrazzo floor utilizes this cheap version of marble to stylish effect. It was reopened in 1982 and is now owned by singer Gloria Estefan.

10 Cavalier Hotel
A traditional Art Deco hotel *(left)*, which provides quite a contrast to the later Cardozo next door. Where the Cardozo emphasizes the horizontal and vaguely nautical, this façade is starkly vertical and temple-like. The temple theme is enhanced by beautifully ornate vertical stucco friezes, which recall the abstract, serpentine geometric designs of the Aztecs and other Meso-American cultures.

For details about staying at SoBe's Art Deco hotels See p147

Striking motifs on Tropical Deco buildings

Tropical Deco Features

1 Tropical Motifs
These include Florida palms and panthers, orchids and alligators, but especially birds, such as flamingos and cranes.

2 Ice-Cream Colors
Actually, most Deco buildings here were originally white, with a bit of painted trim; the present-day rich pastel palette "Deco Dazzle" was the innovation of Miami designer and Capitman collaborator Leonard Horowitz in the 1980s.

3 Nautical Features
What better way to remind visitors of the ocean and its pleasures than with portholes and ship-railings? Some of the buildings resemble beached liners.

4 Curves and Lines
This suggestion of speed is the essence of the Streamline Moderne style – it is an implicit appreciation of the power of technology.

5 Stucco Bas-Relief Friezes
These sculptural bands offered designers endless possibilities for a wonderful mix of ancient and modern motifs and themes.

6 Stylized, Geometric Patterning
This was a nod to the extreme modernity of Cubism, as well as, again, the power and precision of technology espoused by Bauhaus precepts.

Sunburst motif, Cardozo

7 Fantasy Towers
Many Deco buildings try to give the viewer a sense of something mythical – towers that speak of far shores or exalted visions – and that effectively announce the hotel's name, as well.

8 Neon
Used mostly for outlining architectural elements, neon lighting, in a glamorous range of colors, came into its own with Tropical Deco.

9 Chrome
What touch more perfectly says "modern" than a cool, incorruptible silver streak? Chrome is used as detailing on and within many buildings.

10 Glass Blocks
Used in the construction of many Deco walls, the glass blocks give a sense of light and lightness in a part of the country where indoor-outdoor living is year-round.

"Aztec" frieze, Cavalier

For other architectural wonders in and around Miami See pp46–7

Top 10 Architects

1. **Henry Hohauser** Park Central, Colony, Edison, Cardozo, Governor, Essex, Webster, Century, Taft
2. **Albert Anis** Clevelander, Waldorf, Avalon, Majestic, Abbey, Berkeley Shore, Olympic
3. **Anton Skislewicz** Breakwater, Kenmore
4. **L. Murray Dixon** Tiffany, Palmer House, Fairmont, Tudor, Senator, St. Moritz
5. **Igor B. Polevitsky** Shelborne
6. **Roy F. France** Cavalier
7. **Robert Swartburg** Delano, The Marseilles
8. **Kichnell & Elliot** Carlyle
9. **Henry O. Nelson** Beacon
10. **Russell Pancoast** Bass Museum

Deco Dazzle
In the 1980s, some 150 buildings were colored by Leonard Horowitz, to the dismay of purists.

The Story of Tropical Deco

The Art Deco style took the world stage following the 1925 Exposition in Paris, synthesizing all sorts of influences, from Art Nouveau's flowery forms, Bauhaus, and Egyptian imagery to the geometric patterns of Cubism. In 1930s America, Art Deco buildings reflected the belief that technology was the way forward, absorbing the speed and edginess of

Streamline Moderne

the Machine Age as well as the fantasies of science fiction and even a tinge of ancient mysticism. The thrilling new style was just what was needed to counteract the gloom of the Great Depression and give Americans a coherent vision for the future. In Miami, the style was exuberantly embraced and embellished upon with the addition of numerous local motifs, becoming "Tropical Deco." Its initial glory days were not to last long, however. Many hotels became soldiers' barracks in World War II and were torn down afterward. Fortunately, Barbara Baer Capitman fought a famous battle to preserve the buildings. The Miami Beach Historic District was designated in 1979.

Calle Ocho, Little Havana

Cubans live all over South Florida, but Little Havana has been their surrogate homeland since they first started fleeing Cuba in the 1960s. Don't expect much in the way of sights in this district – your time here is most profitably spent out in the streets, soaking up the atmosphere. The heart of the area is Southwest 8th Street, better known by its Spanish name, Calle Ocho. Its liveliest stretch, between SW 11th and SW 17th avenues, is best enjoyed on foot, but other points of interest are more easily reached by car.

Eternal flame

Mural on Calle Ocho

🚶 You will have a much easier time in this district if you can speak a good bit of Spanish, especially in shops or when phoning establishments.

🍽 The Versailles (no. 6) is an unmissable part of the Little Havana experience. The neophyte's sampler of Cuban food includes croquettes, roast pork, and sweet plantains.

Map J–M 2–3 • El Crédito 1106 SW 8th St, at SW 11th Ave, 305-858-4162 • Cuban Museum of the Americas, 1300 SW 12th Ave, at SW 13th St, South of Calle Ochohotel, 305-858-8006, Noon-6pm Tue–Fri, donation requested • Versailles Restaurant, 3555 SW 8th St, at SW 35th Ave, 305-444-0240 • $$

Top 10 Attractions

1. El Crédito
2. The Brigade 2506 Memorial on Cuban Memorial Blvd
3. Domino Park
4. Plaza de la Cubanidad
5. Cuban Museum of the Americas
6. Versailles Restaurant
7. Botánica El Aguila Vidente
8. Calle Ocho Walk of Fame
9. Woodlawn Cemetery
10. José Martí Riverfront Park

1 El Crédito
Authentic cigar factory *(above)* and store selling the famous La Gloria Cubana brand. The leaves are grown in the Dominican Republic, reputedly from Cuban tobacco seeds.

3 Domino Park
For decades, male Cubans have gathered at the corner of SW 15th Ave to match wits over intense games of dominoes *(right)*. The pavilion and patio were built to accommodate the players in 1976.

Botánica shop front in Little Havana

2 The Brigade 2506 Memorial on Cuban Memorial Boulevard
An eternal flame *(top)* honors the Cuban-Americans who died in the Bay of Pigs invasion of Cuba in 1961. Other memorials pay tribute to Cuban heroes Antonio Maceo and José Martí, who fought against Spanish colonialism in the 1800s.

For more Latino arts venues, shops, and restaurants See pp87–9

Plaza de la Cubanidad

At the Plaza is a bronze map of Cuba and a flourish of banners *(above)* for the headquarters of Alpha 66, Miami's most hard-line anti-Castro group.

5 Cuban Museum of the Americas

The museum has a collection of works by Cuban and other Hispanic artists, and stages temporary exhibitions about Latin-American culture. Some exhibitions of pro-Castro Cuban artists have caused controversy.

8 Calle Ocho Walk of Fame

One of the few real sights that Little Havana has to offer the casual tourist. Imitating Hollywood, pink marble stars embedded in the sidewalks *(above)* recognize not only Cuban celebrities, beginning with salsa singer Celia Cruz in 1987, but also all famous Hispanics with any ties to South Florida.

9 Woodlawn Cemetery

Here lie the remains of two former Cuban presidents, dictator Gerardo Machado, as well as Nicaraguan dictator Anastasio Somoza. There's also the founder of the Cuban American National Foundation.

10 José Martí Riverfront Park

This small, pretty park, lying partly under I-95, was dedicated in 1985 to commemorate the Cuban struggle for freedom. The site became a Tent City for many of the 125,000 homeless Mariel boatlift refugees in 1980.

6 Versailles Restaurant

A trip to Miami is incomplete without at least a snack at this legendary institution. It's a Cuban version of a fancy diner, with mirrors everywhere and a constant hubbub.

7 Botánica El Aguila Vidente

Santería is a Cuban religion, combining Catholicism, the Yoruba culture of Nigeria, and Native American practices. This *botánica* is one of several establishments offering paraphernalia and spiritual consultations.

Top 10 Cuban Cultural Imports

1. Cigars
2. Salsa, mambo, bolero, merengue (rhythms)
3. Santería (mystical belief system)
4. Spanish language
5. Cafecito (Cuban coffee)
6. Black beans and plantains
7. Guayabera shirts
8. Gloria Estefan
9. The Buena Vista Social Club (movie)
10. Before Night Falls (movie)

TOP10 Villa Vizcaya

A trumped-up pastiche it may be, but Villa Vizcaya is undeniably grand and glorious, with the authentic feel of a 16th-century Italian palace. Which is exactly what its makers, industrial magnate James Deering, designer Paul Chalfin, and architect F. Burrall Hoffman, intended when they built it in the early 1900s. Embodying a 400-year range of styles, both the genuine and ersatz have been skillfully assembled to evoke another culture, another continent, and another age.

The Villa and its formal gardens

Venetian-style building

🌀 Take the guided tour for lots of juicy gossip about Mr. Deering's posh ways, as well as various legends, superstitions and quirks about many of the furnishings.

🌀 The museum café, located at the left end of the villa, is a pleasant culinary surprise.

Map L6 • 3251 South Miami Ave • 305-250-9133 • www.vizcaya museum.com
• 9:30am–4:30pm daily
• House closes at 5pm, gardens at 5:30pm
• Closed Christmas Day
• Adm $10; children 6–12 $5; 5 & under free

Top 10 Sights
1. Gardens
2. East Loggia
3. Italian Renaissance Living Room
4. Rococo Music Room
5. Breakfast Room
6. Empire Bathroom
7. Italian Renaissance Dining Room
8. French Rococo Reception Room
9. Neoclassical Entrance Hall and Library
10. Swimming Pool Grotto

1 Gardens
The villa's gardens, although somewhat neglected, will probably give you the greatest pleasure. The many splashing fountains of gracefully carved stone, statuary *(right)*, and cleverly laid-out formal plantings offer myriad harmonious and ever-changing vistas. The Secret Garden conceals the greatest artistry.

2 East Loggia
This portico frames magnificent views of the sea and of the quaint breakwater known as the Barge. Carved in the shape of a large ship, it provides a perfect foreground to Key Biscayne, lying off the coast.

3 Italian Renaissance Living Room
The room includes a 2,000-year-old marble Roman tripod, a 15th-century Hispano-Mooresque rug, a tapestry depicting the *Labors of Hercules*, and a Neapolitan altar screen.

4 Rococo Music Room
All flowers and fluff, the room *(left)* is graced with an exquisite Italian harpsichord from 1619, a dulcimer, and a harp.

5 Breakfast Room
Four massive ceramic Chinese Foo dogs guard the steps that ascend to what is probably the most bombastic room in the house.

6 Empire Bathroom
Few bathrooms in the world are more ornate than this marble, silver, and gilded affair *(below)*. The bathtub was designed to run either fresh- or salt-water from the Bay of Biscayne.

8 French Rococo Reception Room
The assemblage is a mix of styles, but the overall look is of a salon under the 18th-century French King Louis XV. The tinted plaster ceiling is from the Rossi Palace in Venice.

7 Italian Renaissance Dining Room
Another echo of the antique Italian taste, featuring a 2,000-year-old Roman table, a pair of 16th-century tapestries, and a full set of 17th-century chairs.

Key
■ First floor
■ Second floor
■ Gardens

9 Neoclassical Entrance Hall and Library
Though still 18th-century, the mood is considerably more sober in these rooms, which are in the English Neoclassical style, inspired by the work of Robert Adam.

10 Swimming Pool Grotto
In imitation of Italian Renaissance and Baroque architects, who were in turn imitating ancient Roman styles, this pool *(above)* extends under the house and resemble a natural cave or sea grotto.

Deering's Dream
Money was no object for industrialist James Deering. He wanted his winter residence to provide a sense of family history as well as luxury. Thus he bought up bits of European pomp, shipped them over, and reassembled them on this ideal spot by the sea.

Merrick's Coral Gables Fantasies

Coral Gables, one of the country's richest neighborhoods, is a separate city within Greater Miami, and feels it. Aptly described as the City Beautiful, its swanky homes line avenues shaded by giant banyans and oak, backing up to hidden canals. Regulations ensure that new buildings use the same architectural vocabulary advocated by George Merrick when he planned the community in the 1920s. Merrick's taste sometimes ran to the Disneyesque, but undeniably he created a wonderland of a place that has not lost its aesthetic impact.

Chinese Village

George Merrick

🚗 Driving around Coral Gables can be tricky. Many of the streets have two names, and the signs are spelled out on stucco blocks at ground level, which can be hard to read, especially at night.

🍴 Sample the excellent salads and soups at Books and Books, on 265 Aragon Ave, where you can also delve deeper into local history.

Map F–G 3–4

Top 10 Sights

1. Biltmore Hotel
2. Venetian Pool
3. Chinese Village
4. Congregational Church
5. Dutch South African Village
6. French Normandy Village
7. French Country Village
8. French City Village
9. Italian Village
10. Florida Pioneer Village

1 Biltmore Hotel
Merrick's masterpiece has been refurbished and burnished to its original splendor, at a cost of more than $55 million *(below)*. Built in 1926, it remains one of the most stunning hotels in the country. It served as a military hospital during World War II and was a veteran's hospital until 1968. The 315-ft (96-m) near-replica of Seville's Giralda Tower is a Coral Gables landmark *(see also the Freedom Tower, p83)*.

2 Venetian Pool
The boast that this is the most beautiful swimming pool in the world is a fair one *(above & p99)*. Incorporating waterfalls and a cave, it was fashioned from a coral rock quarry in 1923 by Merrick's associates, Denman Fink and Phineas Paist.

3 Chinese Village
An entire block has been transformed into a walled Chinese enclave. The curved, glazed-tile roofs peek above the trees in vibrant colors, with Chinese red and yellow, and bamboo motifs predominating.

For more on Coral Gables and the neighboring Coconut Grove district **See pp98–105**

Congregational Church

Coral Gables' first church *(above)*, built by Merrick in the Spanish Baroque style, is actually a replica of a church in Costa Rica.

5 Dutch South African Village

Northern Baroque frivolity meets hot-weather practicality. This charming collection of homes embodies the high-peaked façades and scrolls of typical Dutch architecture, along with the white stucco walls and red roofs associated with the Mediterranean. The style evolved as Boers adapted to African climes.

6 French Normandy Village

The most homogeneous of all the Villages at Coral Gables, this is all open timberwork, white stucco, and shake (cedar) roofs. Little alcoves and gardens here and there complete the picture-postcard look.

7 French Country Village

Seven mansions are built in various styles typical of the French countryside. Some have open timber, stone, red brick, and shake (cedar) roofs, others resemble the classic grange. One sports a marvelous turret.

8 French City Village

Here you'll find a series of nine graceful *petits palais* in the grand French style, looking almost as if a city block of Paris has been airlifted over. The most elaborate confection is on the north corner of Cellini and Hardee.

9 Italian Village

The typical country type of Italian villa, with its red tile roof and painted stucco walls. Many later constructions have carried on the theme, so the original Merrick creations are almost lost in the mix.

10 Florida Pioneer Village

Imitations of the early plantation and colonial homes built by Florida's first aristocrats. The style incorporates Neoclassical, columned porches with the stucco walls of tropical tradition.

Merrick the Visionary

Merrick's dream was to build an American Venice. The massive project spawned the biggest real estate venture of the 1920s, costing around $100 million. The hurricane of 1926 then the Wall Street crash of 1929 left Merrick's city incomplete and him destitute, but what remains of his vision is an enduring testament to his imagination.

Want to tour the Biltmore or even stay there? **See pp99 & 146**

📖 Lowe Art Museum

Originally founded in 1925, with the aid of a $5-million endowment from George Merrick (see p19), the Lowe was reorganized in 1950–52 thanks to a donation from philanthropists Joe and Emily Lowe, and it has since become Miami's premier art museum. More than 12,000 pieces showcase many of the world's most important artistic traditions. Collectors keep on donating works so that even more expansion to the galleries is now necessary to display them all. Nevertheless, the most significant works are always on display, unless on loan to other museums.

Museum exterior

🛍 Check the museum store for a wide array of beautifully illustrated books on the Lowe collection.

🍴 A local favorite, the Titanic Brewing Company (5813 Ponce de Leon Blvd, 305-667-2537) serves up seafood, live music, and six kinds of hand-crafted ale.

Map F3 • 1301 Stanford Drive • 305-284-3535 • www.lowemuseum.org • 10am–5pm Tue, Wed, Fri, Sat; noon–7pm Thu; noon–5pm Sun • Closed Mon and national holidays • Adm $5; concessions $3

Top 10 Collections

1. Egyptian
2. Greco-Roman
3. Asian
4. Pre-Columbian
5. Native American
6. Renaissance
7. Baroque
8. Latin-American
9. African
10. 17th–Century to Modern European & American

2 Greco-Roman
Classical sculpture is represented by several marble carvings, including a Roman portrait bust of a matron. One of the best objects is a 6th-century BC black-figure krater *(above)*, depicting Apollo, Artemis, and Leto.

1 Egyptian
The Egyptian collection is tiny but fascinating, especially the Coptic textiles, several intriguing fragments of which are displayed in frames on the wall. There is also a jewel-like portrait sarcophagus mask, intended to resemble the features of the deceased.

3 Asian
One of the Museum's strongest collections, featuring magnificent Chinese Neolithic pots *(left)*, Shang bronzes, Han figures and pottery, T'ang three-color glazed works, and sublime Sung and Yuan porcelains. Japan and Korea are also well represented.

For more fabulous museums in Miami and the Keys See pp42–3

4 Pre-Columbian
An excellent collection covers all eras and areas, from about 1500 BC to the 16th century. A Mayan pot with a jaguar and human bone design is very forceful. The silver disk from 14th-century Peru *(below)* is a very rare piece.

5 Native American
A Seminole shoulder bag *(left)* is the pride of this collection, beautifully executed using thousands of tiny, colored-glass trade beads. The Najavo, Apache, and Hopi art forms include textiles, pottery, basketry, and *kachina* dolls.

6 Renaissance
The small but exquisite collection of mostly Italian paintings includes works by Tintoretto, Dosso Dossi, Palma Vecchio, Bicci di Lorenzo, and Cozzarelli *(right)*. There are also two lovely terra-cottas by Andrea della Robbia.

7 Baroque
This period in European art is epitomized here by painters from many countries, such as Jacob Jordaens, Lucas Cranach the Elder, Jusepe de Ribera, and Francesco Guardi.

8 Latin-American
Important holdings of 20th-century art by Hispanic artists include Fernando Botero of Colombia and Carlos Alfonzo, who was born in Cuba.

9 African
Works as diverse as the 16th-century cast bronze ring of the Yoruba people, depicting ritual decapitation, a Nok terra-cotta figure *(right)*, and an Elpe or Ngbe society emblem assemblage all have an undeniable potency.

10 17th-Century to Modern European & American
Some extraordinary works on permanent display include *Americanoom* by Chryssa, *Modular Painting in Four Panels* by Roy Lichtenstein, *Le Neveu de Rameau* by Frank Stella, *Football Player (left)* by Duane Hanson, and *Rex* by Deborah Butterfield.

Museum Guide
The Lowe is located in the middle of the campus of the University of Miami, which is in southern Coral Gables and is easily accessible by the Miami Metrorail – just follow the signs. There is no particular order in which you are expected to visit the collections. Remember that several of the galleries are always given over to special temporary exhibitions.

🔟 The Wolfsonian

Strangely, the museum began life in the 1920s as the Washington Storage Company – Miami's wealthier winter residents used to store their valuables here when they were away. Eventually, in 1984, one Mitchell Wolfson, Jr. decided to buy it outright as a home for his vast assemblage of the rich detritus of modernity. It opened to the public in 1995. Over 70,000 objects include decorative and propaganda art, furniture, and much, much more.

Façade of Mediterranean-Revival Building

🕐 Ask about the tour that is available upon request and check the museum store for its excellent catalogs.

🔵 In the Moderne mood, the popular Streamline Moderne Diner on 11th St & Washington Ave (305-534-6373) has malted milk shakes and hamburgers, as well as more sophisticated fare.

Map R4 • 1001 Washington Ave, Miami Beach
• 305-531-1001
• www.wolfsonian.org
• 11am–6pm Mon, Tue, Fri, Sat; 11am–9pm Thu; noon–5pm Sun • Closed Wed & national holidays
• Adults $5; concessions $3.50

Top 10 Exhibits

1. Bridge Tender's House
2. Mediterranean-Revival Building
3. Entrance Hall
4. Fountain
5. The Wrestler
6. Art Deco Mail Box
7. Ceiling, Chandeliers, and Brackets
8. Wooden Staircase
9. Clarke Window
10. Temporary Exhibits

1 Bridge Tender's House

Standing just to the north of the Wolfsonian's entrance, this remarkable 1939 building is a stainless-steel hexagonal structure designed in the Art Moderne style.

2 Mediterranean-Revival Building

The Spanish Baroque-style relief around the main entrance is a striking feature. The bronze flagpole brackets and finials date from 1914.

The Wrestler

3 Entrance Hall

The massive ceiling supports *(below)* reflect the Mediterranean-Revival style of the façade and are original to the building. So are the terra-cotta floors, the woodwork over the doors leading to the elevator vestibule, and the rough stucco walls. The stonework is unfinished according to Mediterranean-Revival tenets.

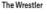

4 Fountain

Set under a skylight, the fountain was fashioned from an elaborate Deco window grille taken from the Norris Theater in Pennsylvania. Composed of over 200 gilded and glazed terra-cotta tiles, the richly floral decorative scheme belies the careful geometrical structure of the piece.

5 The Wrestler

The symbol of the Wolfsonian *(left)* confronts visitors as they approach the elevator. Its brawny, nude, life-sized form is made entirely of aluminum, perhaps the quintessential metal of 20th-century modernity.

8 Wooden Staircase

This fine piece of modern woodcraft *(right)* is fashioned from pine and steel. It came from the Curtis Bok residence, Gulph Mills, Pennsylvania, designed by Wharton Esherick in 1935.

9 Clarke Window

The stained-glass window *(below)* made for the League of Nations' International Labor Building in Geneva, Switzerland, in 1926–30, is an impressive piece.

Key

▩	First floor
▨	Fifth floor
▦	Sixth floor
■	Seventh floor

6 Art Deco Mailbox

To the left of the elevator is a wonderful 1929 Art Deco bronze mailbox *(left)*, originally in New York Central Railroad Terminal, Buffalo.

7 Ceiling, Chandeliers, and Brackets

These unique decorative features come from a 1920s Miami car showroom and a restaurant in Missouri.

10 Temporary Exhibits

Much of the available gallery space is used throughout the year for special exhibits, often with compelling themes that reflect the subjects of research at the University. Propaganda art has featured, showing how savvy designers have called upon the science of psychology to create highly persuasive images for businesses and governments.

Orientation

The Wolfsonian is both a museum and a design research institute attached to Florida International University. Three of the floors are used for offices, storage, and a library, and are not normally open to the public. Your tour should begin outside, progress to the Entrance Hall, then up the back elevator to floors 5, 6, and 7.

Miami's Top 10

TOP 10 Gold Coast Highway A1A

The very best way to get a feel for the quality of life along the Gold Coast is to take a leisurely drive north on A1A. The road hugs the beach almost all the way and passes through some of the most beautiful natural settings and some of the wealthiest communities in the U.S. The 50-mile (80-km) route can be traversed in a day, but it's worth spending more time to take in the local color, from tropical nature preserves to fabulous mansions, all within sight of the sugary blond sands and the azure Atlantic.

John U. Lloyd Park

The Broadwalk

🏀 To get the most out of Fort Lauderdale, take the one-hour Canal Cruise (954-267-3699).

🍽 Lunch in Fort Lauderdale at Noodles Panini, 821 East Las Olas Blvd (954-462-1514). At dinnertime, head for Las Olas Café, 922 East Las Olas Blvd (954-524-4300) or Bistro Mezzaluna, 741 SE 17th St Causeway, (954-522-6620).

Map D2 • Graves Museum, 481 South Federal Highway, Dania Beach (954-925-7770) • Flagler Museum, 1 Whitehall Way, Palm Beach (561-655-2833) • Norton Museum of Art, 1451 S. Olive Ave, West Palm Beach (561-832-5196)

Top 10 Sights

1. The Broadwalk
2. John U. Lloyd Beach State Park
3. South Florida Museum of Natural History
4. Las Olas Boulevard, Fort Lauderdale
5. Bonnet House
6. Gumbo Limbo Nature Center
7. Worth Avenue, Palm Beach
8. Flagler Museum
9. The Breakers
10. Norton Museum of Art

1 The Broadwalk
This famous stretch of Hollywood Beach *(above)* runs from South Sunset Road to Sheridan, where 2.5 miles (4 km) of shops, bars, and restaurants abound, best of all the French-Caribbean fusion of Sugar Reef.

Flagler Museum

2 John U. Lloyd Beach State Park
This long barrier island of gardens and forests commands views of busy Port Everglades and a beach historically significant as one designated for African-Americans, in the days of segregation. It's now a gay destination *(see p52)*.

3 Graves Museum of Archaeology and Natural History
Exhibits here include dinosaur fossils, dioramas of prehistoric Florida, African wood-carvings, Pre-Columbian pottery figures, Minoan bronzes, Egyptian statuary, and Native American collections. The museum's usually a big hit with kids.

Fort Lauderdale has many facilities for gay visitors
See pp52–3 & 153

4 Las Olas Boulevard, Fort Lauderdale

Fort Lauderdale's main street (above) boasts upscale shops and excellent eateries. At the river end, Las Olas Riverfront is a colorful theme mall, from which the Riverfront Canal Cruise departs (see panel).

5 Bonnet House

This period home (built 1920) is full of the personality of the couple who created it, Frederic and Evelyn Bartlett. They were both artists, as is evident from the highly original murals, and the somewhat eccentric tropical gardens.

6 Gumbo Limbo Nature Center

An informative center, with a boardwalk that winds through mangroves and hammocks (raised areas) in Red Reef Park. It takes its name from the gumbo limbo tree, which has distinctive, red peeling bark.

7 Worth Avenue, Palm Beach

The street (above) for local and visiting VIPs to select this week's wardrobe and perhaps a little objet d'art.

9 The Breakers

The third hotel to be built on this site, the first two having burned down. However, the aura of America's Gilded Age (1880–1910) still clings to every aspect of this stylish abode (below), from the frescoed Italianate ceilings to the countless crystal chandeliers.

8 Flagler Museum

The "Taj Mahal of America," was Henry M. Flagler's (see p45) wedding gift to his third wife, who was half his age and an heiress herself. The trappings of royalty are everywhere, down to the hand-painted dinner service that once belonged to a French king.

10 Norton Museum of Art

Perhaps Florida's finest museum of art, featuring Impressionists, Modern Americans, and much more (see p42).

All That Glitters

Here, all that glitters probably is gold! The Gold Coast may have got its name from gold doubloons that Spanish galleons used to carry along the intracoastal waterways, but these days the term refers more to the golden lifestyle of the many millionaires and billionaires who have winter homes here.

Want to continue farther north on A1A? **See p128**

🔟 Key West

First recorded by Spanish explorers in 1513, this tiny island (key), just two miles by four (3.2 x 6.4 km), has changed in status from a pirates' den to the most prosperous city per capita in the US. Always attracting free-thinkers, eccentrics, and misfits, Key West has a uniquely oddball character that is still apparent despite the upscale tourism that has developed since the 1990s. The self-named Conch ("conk") inhabitants include many gays, writers, artists, and New-Agers.

Shipwreck Museum

Sunset, Mallory Square

🚗 You can travel by road from the mainland all the way through the Keys, crossing various bridges, to Key West.

The Conch Tour Train, boarding at Mallory Square, provides an overview of Old Town.

🍴 Rick's Blue Heaven, at 729 Thomas St, is the quintessence of old Key West: a Caribbean menu and a garden with trademark Key West chickens and cats wandering around. *(Also see p125 for the best of Conch dining.)*

Map A6 • Key West Welcome Center, 3840 N. Roosevelt Blvd 1-888-222-5148 • www.keywestinfo.com • Museums 9am–5pm (approx.) daily; adm • Cemetery sunrise–6pm daily; free • Fort Zachary, Taylor 8am–sunset daily; adm

Top 10 Sights

1. Duval Street
2. Mallory Square
3. Bahama Village
4. Mel Fisher's Maritime Heritage Society Museum
5. Hemingway House
6. Audubon House and Tropical Gardens
7. Key West Cemetery
8. Key West Art and History Museum
9. Lighthouse Museum
10. Fort Zachary Taylor State Historic Site

1 Duval Street
Running from the Gulf of Mexico at the north end to the Atlantic Ocean in the south, the main street of Old Town is the place to do the "Duval Crawl." This is the arduous task of strolling the street and stopping in at all of the 100 or so bars, pubs, and clubs that line Duval and its neighboring roads.

2 Mallory Square
Every evening at sunset, the fun-loving citizens of the self-styled "Conch Republic" throw a party in this large, seaside square, complete with entertainers of all sorts.

Duval Street

3 Bahama Village
An archway across Petronia Street at Duval announces that you are entering this largely African-American neighborhood, which offers a tiny slice of Island culture *(left)*. A block in is the Bahama Market, featuring handicrafts; farther along is Rick's Blue Heaven *(see panel)*.

For more on Key West's local architectural style **See p47**

4 Mel Fisher's Maritime Heritage Society Museum

Dedicated to the lure and lore of sunken treasure and the equipment *(left)* that has been used to retrieve it. Most impressive are the gold artifacts from 17th-century Spanish galleons.

Hemingway House 5

"Papa" Ernest Hemingway lived in this Spanish colonial-style house built of coral rock from 1931–40, and wrote many of his works here. Remnants of his stay include boxing gloves *(right)* and supposed descendants of his six-toed cats.

6 Audubon House and Tropical Gardens

A glimpse into mid-19th-century life on the island. The audio tour is excellent, as "ghosts" of the family who lived here take you through the rooms.

7 Key West Cemetery

The tombs are raised to avoid flooding and because the soil is mostly hard coral rock. Famously droll epitaphs include "I told you I was sick" on the tomb of a notorious hypochondriac.

9 Lighthouse Museum

Built in 1848, Key West's lighthouse was capable of beaming light 25 miles (40 km) out to sea. Climb the 88 steps to enjoy panoramic seascapes and views of the town.

8 Key West Art and History Museum

Housed in the imposing old Customs House are paintings of some of the island's eccentrics and notables, along with accounts of life here in various epochs.

10 Fort Zachary Taylor State Historic Site

The 1866 brick fort is now a military museum *(left)* with a fine collection of Civil War artifacts. The island's best beach is nearby.

Top 10 Denizens

1. **Henry Flagler** Standard Oil magnate
2. **José Martí** Cuban freedom fighter
3. **John James Audubon** Naturalist
4. **Ernest Hemingway** Writer
5. **Harry S. Truman** President
6. **Tennessee Williams** Playwright
7. **Robert Frost** Poet
8. **John Dewey** Educator-philosopher
9. **Jimmy Buffett** Singer-songwriter
10. **Tallulah Bankhead** Actress

For a day's itinerary, shops, restaurants, and regular events in Key West See pp117–25

☆10 The Everglades

One of the planet's most fascinating ecosystems, the Everglades is a vast, shallow river system of swamps and wetlands, whose waters can take a year or more to meander from the Kissimmee River, northwest of Miami, into Florida Bay. At least 45 plant varieties grow here that are found nowhere else on Earth. It is also home to over 350 kinds of bird, 500 types of fish, and dozens of reptile and mammal species.

Alligator, Billie Swamp Wildlife Park

Pinelands in the heart of the Everglades

🍃 Try to visit the Everglades early in the morning, when many animals are active. Protect yourself from biting insects, sun, and heat, and keep to the boardwalks.

🍽 The Swamp Water Café on the Big Cypress Reservation (863-983-6101) offers alligator tail nuggets, catfish filets, and frog legs, alongside the usual hamburgers, etc, all at reasonable prices.

Maps B–C 3–5 • Everglades National Park 305-242-7700 • Visitor Center, Everglades City (941) 695-3311 • Big Cypress Swamp: Oasis Visitor Center (941) 695-4111 • Shark Valley Information Center 305-221-8776 • Flamingo Visitor Center (941) 695-2945 • Fakahatchee Strand (941) 695-4593 • Corkscrew Swamp, 375 Sanctuary Rd (941) 657-3771

Top 10 Sights

1. Tamiami Trail (US 41)
2. Everglades National Park
3. Big Cypress Swamp
4. Shark Valley
5. Ah-Tah-Thi-Ki and Billie Swamp
6. Anhinga and Gumbo Limbo Trails
7. Mahogany Hammock
8. Flamingo
9. Fakahatchee Strand
10. Corkscrew Swamp

1 Tamiami Trail (US 41)

This was the first road to open up the area by linking the Atlantic and Gulf coasts. It passes pioneer camps, such as Everglades City and Chokoloskee, which have barely changed since the late 1800s. They mark the western entrance to Everglades National Park.

2 Everglades National Park

The park covers about one-fifth of the Everglades. There are elevated boardwalks, tours, canoe rental, camping and hotel and *chikee* lodgings (Seminole-style huts).

3 Big Cypress Swamp

This vast, shallow wetland basin is not a true swamp but a range of wet and dry habitats determined by slight differences in elevation. It is home to hundreds of species, including the Florida panther.

4 Shark Valley

This area, only 17 miles (27 km) from the western edge of Miami, has a 15-mile (24-km) loop road that you can travel by bicycle or on a narrated tram ride. It ends at a tower *(left)* that affords great views.

5 Ah-Tah-Thi-Ki and Billie Swamp

A museum here is devoted to Native American Seminole culture *(left)* – *ah-tah-thi-ki* means "a place to learn, or remember." A wildlife park nearby has exhilarating airboat rides and informative Buggy Eco-Tours, from which you might spot alligators.

6 Anhinga and Gumbo Limbo Trails

Both of these popular trails begin at the Royal Palm Visitor Center, the site of Florida's first state park.

7 Mahogany Hammock

Farther along toward Flamingo, you'll come to one of the park's largest hammocks (fertile mounds), where a trail meanders through dense tropical growth. This is home to the largest mahogany tree in the country and colorful tree snails.

Preserving the Everglades

The Everglades evolved over a period of more than 6 million years, but humans almost destroyed its fragile balance in less than 100. In the 1920s, the Hoover Dike closed off Lake Okeechobee, the main source of Everglades water, and Highway 41 was built, further blocking its natural flow. Thankfully, environmentalist Marjory Stoneman Douglas reversed the march toward doom. Today, there are plans to build levees around the Everglades, to help keep the vital moisture in.

9 Fakahatchee Strand

One of Florida's wildest areas, a 20-mile (32-km) slough (muddy backwater), noted for the largest stand of native royal palms in the US, unique air plants, and rare orchids. There are boardwalks *(right)* and rangers on hand.

10 Corkscrew Swamp

A boardwalk takes you through various habitats, including a stand of old cypress full of nesting birds. The endangered wood stork has been spotted here.

8 Flamingo

Flamingo is called home by only a handful of park rangers these days, but it was once an outpost for hunters, fishermen, and smugglers, accessible only by water. Sportfishing, canoeing, bird-watching, and hiking are very good here.

For routes through the Everglades and places to eat
See pp127 & 130

Left **South Pointe Beach** Center **Matheson Hammock Beach** Right **Key West**

☝10 Beaches

1 Lummus Park Beach

This broad, long, and well-maintained stretch of sand is, for many, the epitome of South Beach. In season, bronzed bodies line up row after row, some with boom boxes blasting, others just catching the rays. The more active play volleyball, do gymnastics, and, of course, take to the waves. From 5th to 11th Streets, women can go topless. ◈ *Map S3*

2 Haulover Park Beach

Haulover has been spared the sight of high-rise development. The dune-backed beach lies along the eastern side of the park, and to the north it has become the only nude beach in the county, part of it gay. ◈ *Map H2 • Just north of Bal Harbour*

3 South Pointe Park Beach

Though not well known for its beaches, the park's northern part is popular with surfers, and you can watch cruise ships gliding in and out of the Port of Miami.

It's also great for walks, and there's a fitness course, an observation tower, charcoal grills, picnic spots, and playgrounds. ◈ *Map S6*

4 Sunny Isles Beach

More noteworthy for its 1950s' tourist-resort kitsch than for its rocky sand, this strip is popular with older tourists, as well as surfers and sailors. Souvenir shops and hotels indulge in campy architectural fancies, featuring exotic themes along Collins (A1A) between 160th & 185th Streets. ◈ *Map H3*

5 Hobie Island Beach and Virginia Key Beach

While Hobie is popular with windsurfers, Virginia Key – neighbor to Key Biscayne and similarly shrouded in Australian pines – has no residents and few visitors. Under Old South segregation, it was the only Miami beach African-Americans were allowed to use. Once you walk through the vegetation, the

Haulover Park Beach

 South Beach, Miami's best-known stretch, is covered on **pp8–9**

Typical beach in Miami

2-mile (3-km) beach here is fine and relatively empty. Both are excellent for children due to the warm bay waters, but Virginia Key has deep waters and possible undertow. ◈ *Map H3*

Crandon Beach
One of several South Florida beaches that are rated among the top ten in the entire US, this one is on upper Key Biscayne *(see p72)*. ◈ *Map H3–4*

Bill Baggs Cape Florida State Recreation Area
Also rated as one of the top ten beaches in the US, located at the pristine southern tip of Key Biscayne *(see pp72–3)*. ◈ *Map H4*

Matheson Hammock Park Beach
Considerably battered by 1992's Hurricane Andrew, this 100-acre (40-ha) park is making a comeback. Developed in the 1930s by Commodore J. W. Matheson, it features the man-made Atoll Pool, a salt-water swimming pool encircled by sand and palm trees right alongside Biscayne Bay. The tranquil beach

is popular with families and enjoys warm, safe waters surrounded by tropical hardwood forests. Other attractions include walking trails through the mangrove swamp. ◈ *Map G4 • N of Fairchild Tropical Garden*

Bahia Honda State Park
Frequently voted the best beach in the US, Bahia Honda is noted for its perfect sands, great watersports, and exotic tropical forests *(see p117)*. ◈ *Map B6*

Key West Beaches
Key West's relatively modest beaches are lined up along the southern side of the island, stretching from Fort Zachary Taylor State Park in the west to Smathers Beach in the east. The latter is the largest and most popular, but locals favor the former because it's less crowded. For convenience, the beach at the bottom of Duval Street, at the Southernmost Point in the US, is fine, friendly, and full of refreshment options. ◈ *Map A6*

Left **Swimming with turtles** Center **Fort Lauderdale beach** Right **Scuba diving shop**

Snorkeling and Diving

1 John Pennekamp Coral Reef State Park

Many say this park offers some of the best snorkeling in the world. Various boats can also be rented here, or you can take a more leisurely view from a glass-bottomed boat *(see p115)*.

2 Biscayne National Underwater Park

Closer to Miami than John Pennekamp, the Biscayne National Underwater Park has almost as many good snorkeling possibilities. Here you'll find vivid coral reefs to dive among, and mangrove swamps to explore by canoe *(see p108)*.

Looe Key sign

3 Looe Key National Marine Sanctuary

A brilliant coral dive location, and the closest great snorkeling to Key West. Accessible from Bahia Honda State Park *(see p117)*.

Queen angelfish

4 Dry Tortugas National Park

Located almost 70 miles (110 km) west of Key West, these seven islands and their surrounding waters comprise a fantastic park. The snorkeling sights are exceptional, due to the shallow waters and abundance of marine life. You can snorkel directly off the beaches of Fort Jefferson or take one of the trips to the wreck of the *Windjammer*, which sank on Loggerhead Reef in 1907. Tropical fish, lobster, and even goliath grouper can be found *(see p129)*.

5 Key Biscayne Parks

Both Crandon and Bill Baggs Parks have excellent areas for snorkeling, in some of Miami's cleanest, clearest waters *(see pp72–3)*.

6 Fort Lauderdale Waters

Fort Lauderdale has been awarded the Blue Wave Beaches certification for spotless sands and crystal waters, which add up to superior underwater viewing. Many of the most interesting parts of the three-tiered natural reef system here are close to the shore, though most require a short boat ride. In addition, more than 80 artificial reefs have been built to enhance the growth of marine flora and fauna. Ocean Promotion is one of the

*Be safe in the waters – **See p139***

Diving off the Florida Keys

companies organizing snorkeling and scuba trips. ✪ Map D3 • Ocean promotion 954-561-4499, www.florida-adventure.com/ocean promotion

7 Red Reef Park

Boca Raton is famous for its extensive and beautifully maintained parks, and its Red Reef Park offers some of the best beaches and snorkeling in the area. An artificial reef, clearly marked on the park's visitor map, can provide hours of delightful undersea viewing and is suitable for youngsters. The Gumbo Limbo Environmental Education Center is just across the street. ✪ Map D3 • 1400 State Rd A1A, Boca Raton • 8am–10pm daily • 561-393-7815 • www.ci.boca-raton.fl.us

8 Palm Beach

The Breakers and Four Seasons hotels (see p146) both offer snorkeling options along the Palm Beach coast. ✪ Map D2

9 Bahia Honda State Park Waters

The beautiful, sandy beach of Bahia Honda in the Keys – often lauded as one of the best beaches in the US – has good waters for swimming and snorkeling. Equipment rentals are available (see p117).

10 Key West Waters

Take the plunge right off the beach at Fort Zachary Taylor State Park, or join an expedition out to the reefs that lie all around this island (see pp26–7). There are plenty of trips offered by local companies, most of them taking three to four hours in total, including at least an hour and a half of reef time. They usually leave twice a day, at around 9am and again at about 1pm. ✪ Map A6

Beach at Key West

Left **In-line skating** Center **Cycling** Right **Tennis**

🔟 Sports Activities

Beach volleyball

1 Volleyball
On every beach in South Florida, you'll find nets and likely team members ready to go. This is the quintessential beach sport, where taking a tumble in the sand is part of the fun!

2 In-line Skating
Gliding along on little wheels is probably the number one activity for the terminally tanned of South Florida. Down on flaunt-it-all South Beach, you can rent in-line skates or get fitted for your very own pair.

3 Windsurfing and Surfing
Miami has good prevailing winds and both calm and surging waters: so, plenty of scope for good surfing. The Keys tend to be good for windsurfing only, as the surrounding reefs break the big waves.

Surfing

4 Jet-Skiing and Parasailing
Not as challenging as they may appear and, of course, great fun! In Miami, the placid intracoastal waterways are best, but it's the Keys that have the most superlative conditions, especially Key West. ✆ *Sunset Waterports 305-296-2554 • Sebago Watersports 305-292-2411 • Island Water Sports 305-296-1754 • Key Cat 305-294-4515*

5 Boating and Kayaking
Striking out on your own in a kayak, you can explore the colorful waters around the Keys, or slip into the winding mangrove creeks off Florida Bay. While at the other end of the scale, you could climb aboard historic schooners the *Western Union* or the *America*. ✆ *Kayaking 305-296-3212, 305-304-6906, or 305-292-0059 • Schooner trips 305-292-1766 or 305-292-7787*

6 Dolphin Swims
These unforgettable experiences are available at Miami's Seaquarium and all along the Keys *(see pp115–16)*. Be sure to make reservations as much as a month in advance. Otherwise, try a Dolphin Watch. ✆ *Sunny Days Catamarans 305-293-5144*

The top sports activities on Miami Beach and Key Biscayne are listed on **p74**

Boating

7 Bicycling
An excellent way to explore South Beach, Key Biscayne, or Key West. Rental shops abound, and there are a good number of excellent bike trails in the Everglades, too.

8 Fishing
There are any number of companies that will take you deep-sea fishing, while freshwater fishing is good at Amelia Earhart Park or Lake Okeechobee. ◈ *Reward Fleet, at the Miami Beach Marina, 305-372-9470 (www.fishingmiami.com)* • *In Key West 305-304-2483 or 305-304-8888* • *In Fort Lauderdale (954) 525-4665*

Fishing from Miami Beach Marina

9 Golf
No end of opportunities throughout South Florida. Many resorts have their own courses; one of the best in Greater Miami is the Jacaranda Golf Club in Plantation, voted South Florida's Golf Club of the Year. ◈ *Jacaranda Golf Club 954-472-5836 or 1-888-955-1234* • *Sunrise Country Club (954) 742-4333*

10 Tennis
South Floridians love this game, and there are public and private courts everywhere. Key Biscayne is the top choice, of course, where the Nasdaq 100 Open is held every March *(see sidebar)*.

Spectator Sports

1 Football
Miami's contender in the National Football League is the Miami Dolphins. ◈ *Pro Player Stadium , 2269 NW 199th St*

2 Jai Alai
This fast ball game is similar to lacrosse. ◈ *Miami Fronton, 3500 NW 37th Ave*

3 Horse Racing
Mediterranean-style Hialeah is one of the most famous race tracks in the US. ◈ *Hialeah Park, 2200 E 4th Ave*

4 Dog Racing
While running greyhound races part of the year, Flagler has year-round simulcasting of dog and horse races. ◈ *Flagler Dog Track, 401 NW 37th Ave at NW 7th St*

5 Stock-Car Racing
Homestead Miami Speedway hosts several big events every year. ◈ *1 Speedway Blvd*

6 Tennis
The Nasdaq-100 Open is one of the world's biggest non-Grand Slam tournaments. ◈ *Crandon Park, Key Biscayne*

7 Polo
The "Sport of Kings" is well represented in posh Palm Beach County. ◈ *13420 South Shore Blvd, Wellington*

8 Basketball
The Miami Heat calls the American Airlines Arena home. ◈ *601 Biscayne Blvd*

9 Ice Hockey
The Florida Panthers play out by the Everglades. ◈ *1 Panther Parkway, Sunrise*

10 Baseball Spring Training
Florida's climate has made it a favorite spring training site for major league baseball teams. ◈ *Baltimore Orioles in Davie, 8 mi W of Ft. Lauderdale*

Miami's Top 10

The top sports activities in the Keys are listed on p120

Left **Lion Country Safari** Right **Morikami Museum**

🔟 Parks, Gardens, and Zoos

1 Fairchild Tropical Garden

One of the best of South Florida's ravishing tropical gardens *(see p107)*.

2 Parrot Jungle

A thoroughly enjoyable place, recently relocated to Biscayne Bay, with a petting zoo for children to get close to the animals *(see p71)*.

3 Miami Metrozoo

An extremely well-conceived and beautifully maintained animal park, divided into habitats that imitate Australasia, Asia, and Africa. It takes at least three hours to walk around it all (the time is well worth spending), or take the 45-minute tram tour or Zoofari monorail, the price of which is included in the entrance fee *(see p107)*.

Miami Metrozoo

4 Monkey Jungle

Here you have the chance to walk through the apes' own jungle – where you're the one in the cage! *(See p107.)*

5 Lion Country Safari

Besides effective recreations of habitats in Kenya, Zimbabwe, Mozambique, the Kalihari, and the Serengeti, the extensive park also features evocations of an Indian forest and the Great Plains of North America. Drive or take a guided bus tour through over 500 acres (200 ha) of wildlife. ⊗ *2003 Lion Country Safari Road, Loxahatchee • Map C2–D3 • 561-793-1084 • www.lioncountrysafari.com • Adm*

6 Fruit & Spice Park

The only tropical botanical garden of its kind in the United States. The plants are grouped

Fairchild Tropical Garden

Many of Miami's luxury and resort hotels have stunning topical gardens – **See pp146 & 148**

by country of origin, and the tropical climate here sustains over 100 varieties of citrus plant, 65 of banana, and 40 of grape. The park also houses the largest bamboo collection in the US. In the store you'll find imported fruit products, including dried and canned fruit, juices, jams, teas, and unusual seeds *(see p109)*.

7 Red Reef Park

This wonderful park in Boca Raton contains the Gumbo Limbo Center, which offers nature walks over a coastal hammock (raised area). There is also an artificial reef *(see p33)*.

8 Morikami Museum and Japanese Gardens

Blossoming from a Japanese colony founded here in 1905, the Yamato-kan villa is surrounded by formal Japanese gardens of various ages: a Heian (9th- to 12th-century) *shinden*-style garden, a paradise garden emulating those of the 13th–14th centuries, rock gardens, a flat garden, and a modern romantic garden. Serenity and restraint amid the tropical effusiveness of South Florida. ✪ *4000 Morikami Park Road, Delray Beach • Map D3 • 561-495-0233 • www.morikami.org • Adm*

9 Flamingo Gardens

These beautiful gardens began life in 1927 as a weekend retreat for the citrus-farming Wray family. The lush botanical gardens and bird sanctuary are worth at least half a day. There's a "free-flight" aviary, featuring a mass of Florida birds, including the comical roseate spoonbill and, of course, the flamingo. The rare bald eagle has also made a home here. ✪ *3750 South Flamingo Rd, Davie/Fort Lauderdale • Map D3 • 954-473-2955 • www.flamingogardens.org • Adm*

Flamingo Gardens

10 Nancy's Secret Garden

Lose yourself, or perhaps find yourself, in this impossibly lush acre of land just a block off Duval Street. Intensely beautiful, the garden emanates a palpable sense of peace and contentment. The ravishing varieties of flora – orchids, bromeliads, rare palms – and the well-loved parrots put any visitor at ease. ✪ *1 Free-School Lane, off Simonton, between Fleming and Southard • 305-294-0015 • Adm*

Left **Performance at the Colony** Center **Lincoln Theater** Right **Florida Grand Opera**

🔟 Lively Arts

1 Colony Theater
Starting out as an Art Deco movie theater in 1934, the Colony is now a state-of-the-art venue for some of the city's best classical music concerts, dance, theatrical performances, and experimental film. ⓢ *1040 Lincoln Rd, at Lenox Ave, South Beach • Map Q2 • 305-674-1040*

Ballerina, Miami City Ballet

2 Tropigala
The ambience is a nostalgic recreation of Old Havana clubs before the 1960s, when the Cuban city was a pleasure zone for the free-spending and fast-living. Latin American superstars often feature, though most of the shows are indistinguishable from their Las Vegas counterparts. ⓢ *4441 Collins Ave, Miami Beach • 305-672-7469 • www.clubtropigala.com*

3 Jackie Gleason Theater of the Performing Arts
The theater is unmistakable for its electric blue color and Lichtenstein's *Mermaid* outside.

This is the main Miami venue for top-drawer productions on tour. ⓢ *1700 Washington Ave, South Beach • Map R2 • 305-673-7300 • www.gleasontheater.com*

4 Miracle Theater
The 1940s Deco-style movie theater was converted into a playhouse in 1995 and was soon winning accolades for musicals such as *West Side Story*. ⓢ *280 Miracle Mile, Coral Gables • 305-444-9293 • www.actorsplayhouse.org*

5 Coconut Grove Playhouse
In 1956, Samuel Beckett's *Waiting for Godot* premiered at this restored 1920s venue. Nothing so history-making has since occured, but the likes of Kathleen Turner and Jimmy Buffett perform. ⓢ *3500 Main Highway • 305-442-4000*

6 Miami City Ballet
This is a world-class ballet company, under the direction of Edward Villella. The repertoire

Jackie Gleason Theater of the Performing Arts

Miami City Ballet venue

consists of some 85 ballets.
⊗ 2200 Liberty Ave, Miami Beach • 305-929-7010 • www.miamicityballet.org

7 Florida Grand Opera
The opera house sometimes brings global luminaries to Miami, but their programs also feature new works, such as the compelling *Balseros*, based on the trials of Cuban refugees who attempt to reach Florida by raft.
⊗ 1200 Coral Way • 1-800-741-1010
• www.fgo.org

8 Gusman Center for the Performing Arts
The major Downtown venue offers a program of plays, music, dance, and film (see p84).

9 Lincoln Theater
The Lincoln is home to the New World Symphony, which is made up of music college graduates. The young virtuosos perform an incredible mix of gospel, Piazzolla tango, symphonies, and chamber works. ⊗ 555 Lincoln Rd, South Beach • Map R2 • 305-673-3330 • www.nws.org

10 Miami-Dade County Auditorium
Built in 1951, this Deco-style venue is proud to have been one of the first in the country to host Luciano Pavarotti when he was still a virtual unknown. Operas, concerts, and touring events all benefit from the excellent acoustics in the auditorium. ⊗ 2901 W Flagler St • 305-547-5414

Top 10 Entertainers

1 Jackie Gleason
"The Great One," who practically invented early American television, brought his *Jackie Gleason Show* permanently to Miami in 1964.

2 Don Johnson
Miami Vice-roy himself, the King of 1980s Cool helped put hip "new" South Beach on the map (see p72).

3 Cher
You can see where the ageless diva and Sonny lived on the water in Fort Lauderdale and South Beach.

4 Madonna
She had a palatial spread next to Vizcaya for a while, and still owns a piece of the Delano Hotel restaurant.

5 Dave Barry
The newspaper humorist and author has helped to create Miami's image as an over-the-top urban free-for-all.

6 Gloria Estefan
For many, the symbol of unstoppable Cuban Power, this talented pop songstress has succeeded in building an impressive cultural and real-estate empire.

7 Rosie O'Donnell
The talkshow hostess calls Miami home and is involved in local politics (see also p49).

8 Cameron Diaz
A frequent visitor to South Beach, where she co-owns the Bambú restaurant.

9 Ricky Martin
Another Latino superstar who owns real estate here (Casa Salsa, see p50).

10 Tito Puente, Jr.
The talented musician son of the famed Latin bandleader makes South Florida home, where he promotes gay causes.

Miami's Top 10

For the best Latino arts venues **See p87**

For the best Latino arts venues **See p87**

Left **Coconut Grove Arts Festival** Center **Dade County Fair** Right **International Mango Festival**

🔟 Festivals

1 Key West Fantasy Fest

For two weeks leading up to Halloween, Key West gives itself over to non-stop celebration. Then, on the Saturday before the 31st, a parade, featuring lavish floats and outlandish costumes, departs from Mallory Square and slowly winds down Duval Street. In a spirit of free abandon, many revelers go nude, except for a bit of body paint here and a feather or two there. Ⓢ *Map A6 • Last 2 weeks in Oct*

2 Carnaval Miami

For the Cuban district, March is a time of dancing and singing in the streets – to Latin jazz, pop, flamenco and tango. It culminates on the second Sunday with what claims to be the largest party in the world. Twenty-three blocks of Little Havana are closed off and performers line the way, along

Winter Party

with food stalls of ethnic favorites. An enormous fireworks display brings a resounding finale to the festivities. Ⓢ *8th St from 4th–27th Aves • Map K3 • Approx first ten days of Mar*

3 Winter Party and White Party

These annual gay beach parties are principally about buff young wannabes chasing international-circuit models. Still, one appreciative participant praised the events as "a sea of beautiful, naked men." Well, not entirely naked, but nearly so. Pumped-up raves go on all night in the choicest South Beach venues. Ⓢ *Map R4 • Winter Party first 10 days in Mar; White Party late Nov*

4 Coconut Grove Arts Festival

The Grove *(see pp98–105)* comes fully alive with one of the biggest arts festivals in the country, complete with competitions, all-day concerts, tasty street food, and throngs of avid arts lovers. Ⓢ *Map G3 • 3rd weekend in Feb*

5 Miami-Dade County Fair and Exposition

A traditional American county fair, replete with rides, side-shows, cotton candy, candied apples, live performances, and exhibits relating to farm life and crafts. Ⓢ *Tamiami Park, Coral Way & SW 112th Ave, West Dade • for 18 days from 3rd Thu in Mar*

Carnaval Miami

Key West also hosts delightful, if obscure, events such as conch-blowing and Hemingway Days – See p121

Italian Renaissance Festival

Top 10 Ethnic Attractions

1 **Little Havana**
A little slice of Cuba *(see pp14–15)*.

2 **Little Managua**
Nicaraguan shops abound in the zone (also called Sweetwater) west of Calle Ocho.

3 **Little Haiti**
Come to check out a quirky botánica or two *(see pp91)*.

4 **Billie Swamp Safari Wildlife Center**
The Seminole didactic style is "laugh & learn" *(see p29)*.

5 **Ah-Tah-Thi-Ki Museum**
Exhibits on camp life, ceremonies, and the Seminole economy *(see p29)*.

6 **Miccosukee Indian Village**
Basket-weaving, palmetto doll-making, beadwork, dugout carving, and alligator wrestling.
✎ *US 41, E of Forty Mile Bend • 9am–5pm daily • Adm*

7 **Overtown Historic Village**
The African-American neighborhood has restored some historic buildings such as Dorsey House, at 250 NW 9th St.

8 **Lyric Theater**
Now a reborn venue for African-American cultural events. ✎ *819 NW 2nd Ave, Overtown*

9 **Liberty City**
Site of deadly race riots in 1980, this African-American neighborhood has many interesting murals and graffiti-inspired art.

10 **Historic Homestead Museum and Around**
Most of the historic downtown area has been restored – get a map from the museum.
✎ *41-43 North Krome Ave*

6 **Miami-Bahamas Goombay Festival**
Celebrating Coconut Grove's Bahamian heritage, with music, dance, and loads of fun. ✎ *Map G3 • Usually Oct*

7 **King Mango Strut**
A Coconut Grove spoof on the now-defunct Orange Bowl Parade. ✎ *Map G3 • Last week of Dec*

8 **Hispanic Heritage Festival**
This is a month-long Latino blast, comprising street parties, food festivals, films, music and dance performances, and even an Hispanic beauty pageant. ✎ *Throughout Miami-Dade County • October*

9 **Italian Renaissance Festival**
Renaissance palace gardens provide the perfect venue for this historical-fantasy event – held at must-see Vizcaya *(see pp16–17)*. ✎ *Map L6 • Mar*

10 **International Mango Festival**
The luscious fruit is celebrated with gusto. Enjoy a complete mango feast and learn how to divine when the exotic fruit is at its peak. ✎ *Fairchild Tropical Gardens • Map G4 • Second weekend of Jul*

Left **Lowe Art Museum** Center **Wolfsonian Museum** Right **Historical Museum**

🔟 Museums

1 Lowe Art Museum
Undoubtedly Miami's top art museum, featuring extraordinary works from European, American, Chinese, Pre-Columbian, and Native American cultures *(see pp20–21)*.

2 The Wolfsonian
The perfect complement to the unique Deco District, this is a museum and design research institute with over 70,000 modern design exhibits *(see pp22–3)*.

3 Bass Museum of Art
A collection of Western fine art and design, and historical pictures of Miami Beach *(see p71)*.

4 Norton Museum of Art
One of South Florida's finest, its European collection displays works by Rembrandt, Goya, Renoir, and Picasso. Americans include O'Keeffe and Pollock, and the museum also has strong ancient Chinese and Pre-Columbian collections. 🖲 *1451 S Olive Ave, West Palm Beach • Map D2 • 561-832-5196 • www.norton.org • 10am–5pm Tue–Sat, noon–5pm Sun • Adm*

5 Miami Art Museum
Besides impressive temporary shows, MAM's collection focuses on art since the 1940s, and includes works by Frankenthaler, Gottleib, Rauschenberg, and Stella. 🖲 *101 W Flagler St • Map M2 • 305-375-3000 • www.miamiartmuseum.org • 10am–5pm Tue–Fri, noon–5pm Sat–Sun • Adm*

6 Cuban Museum of the Americas
Hispanic and Caribbean artists are shown here, as well as exhibitions relating to aspects of Cuban culture *(see p15)*.

7 Historical Museum of Southern Florida
Starting as far back in prehistory as 10,000 years, the museum slips swiftly through the millennia

Left **Bass Museum of Art** Right **Norton Museum of Art**

Miami Art Museum

to reach Spanish colonization, Seminole culture, extravagance in the "Roaring Twenties," and Cuban immigration in more recent years. ✆ *101 West Flagler St • Map N2 • 305-375-1492 • www.historical-museum.org • 10am–5pm Mon–Sat (til 9pm Thu), noon–5pm Sun • Adm*

Sanford L. Ziff Jewish Museum of Florida
With its stained-glass windows (one in memory of gangster Meyer Lansky) and Deco details, the synagogue itself is as fascinating as the exhibits it houses. The 230-year Jewish presence in Florida is amply covered. ✆ *301 Washington Ave., South Beach • Map R5 • 305-672-5044 • www.jewishmuseum. com • 10am–5pm Tue–Sun • Adm*

Ah-Tah-Thi-Ki Museum
This excellent museum features Seminole artifacts, such as pottery and beautiful clothing. The Green Corn Ceremony is explained also, including the games, music, dance, and costumes involved. Outside, a nature trail leads through the cypress canopy, where signs explain the use of certain flora in Seminole culture *(see p29)*.

Maritime Museum of the Florida Keys
The romance of long-lost, booty-laden shipwrecks *(see p115)*.

Top 10 Contemporary Collections

1 Rubell Family Collection
About 1,000 works by modern artists, including Haring, Koons, Basquiat, and Cuban artist José Bedia. ✆ *95 NW 29th St*

2 Margulies Collection
Important photography collection, favoring straightforward portraiture. ✆ *591 NW 27th St*

3 Ambrosino Gallery
Work by artists Pablo Soria, William Cordova, and Barbara Strasen. ✆ *769 NE 125th St*

4 Kevin Bruk Gallery, Miami
Featuring work by New York artists Max Gimblett and John Yau. ✆ *3900 NE 1st Ave*

5 Bernice Steinbaum Gallery, Miami
The work of Edouard Duval Carrie and Wendy Wischer. ✆ *3550 N. Miami Ave*

6 Artspace/Virginia Miller Galleries
US and Latin American photographers and artists. ✆ *169 Madeira Ave, Coral Gables*

7 Locust Projects
Specializing in computer-aided and video work by local artists. ✆ *105 NW 23rd St*

8 Barbara Gillman Gallery
Showcasing the work of selected young local artists. ✆ *5582 NE 4th Court, No.5*

9 Casas Riegner
Work by Gustavo Lopez Armentia and other local Latinos. ✆ *23 NE 39th St*

10 Fredric Snitzer Gallery
New collage paintings, featuring the work of Sandy Winters. ✆ *3078 SW 38th Ct*

Left **Coral Castle** Center **Spanish Monastery** Right **Opa-Locka**

10 Historic Sites and Monuments

1 Vizcaya
James Deering's opulent monument celebrating Western civilization and its rich artistic traditions has become Miami's most beloved social and cultural center *(see pp16–17)*.

2 Ancient Spanish Monastery
Originally built in 1133–41 in Segovia, Spain, this monastic building was bought by William Randolph Hearst in 1925 and shipped to New York. The parts were eventually reassembled here in 1952, though, curiously, a few pieces were left over *(see p91)*.

3 The Barnacle
Built in 1891, this is Dade County's oldest house, which cleverly uses ship-building techniques to make it storm proof as well as comfortable (without the use of air-conditioning) in Florida's steamy climate *(see p100)*.

4 Coral Gables Merrick House
The house where the Merrick family lived in the late 1800s and where George Merrick, Coral Gables' master builder, grew up. The contrast between the modest surroundings of his home and the spectacle of his grandiose dreams is fascinating *(see pp18–19)*.

5 Coral Castle
This monument to unrequited love speaks volumes about early Florida's place in US history as a refuge for misfits, eccentrics, and visionaries. Land was cheap (the creator of Coral Castle bought his acre plot for $12 in 1920) and the population was sparse, so it was easy to do your own thing without being bothered. But how this gargantuan folly was actually constructed remains an enigma *(see p108)*.

6 Brigade 2506 Memorial
Little Havana's Eternal Flame and monument garden remembers those who died in the Bay of Pigs debacle, attempting to reclaim Cuba from leftist revolutionary forces in 1961 *(see p14)*.

7 Holocaust Memorial
Miami has one of the largest populations of Holocaust survivors in the world, so this stunning monument has extra poignancy. Sculpted by Kenneth Treister and finished in 1990, the centerpiece is an enormous bronze forearm bearing a stamped number from Auschwitz. The arm is thronged with nearly 100 life-sized figures in attitudes of suffering. The surrounding plaza has a graphic pictorial history of the Holocaust, and a granite wall listing the names of thousands of

Holocaust Memorial

For Miami's historic Art Deco District **See pp10–13**

concentration camp victims.
🅢 *1933-45 Meridian Ave, South Beach*
• *305-538-1663* • *www.holocaustmmb.org*

8 Opa-Locka

Despite the rather seamy area it inhabits, "The Baghdad of Dade County" is worth visiting for its 90 or so Moorish-style buildings. They were built here by Glenn Curtiss during the 1920s boom *(see p91)*.

9 Charles Deering Estate

James Deering's half-brother built this winter residence for himself on Biscayne Bay. The original 19th-century house, Richmond Cottage, was destroyed by Hurricane Andrew in 1992, but it's been rebuilt and the entire estate refurbished since then, including the extraordinary Mediterranean-Revival mansion *(see p107)*.

Stranaham House

10 Stranahan House

Fort Lauderdale's oldest house, built originally in 1901 as a trading post for the Seminoles. The handsome two-story riverside house is furnished with period antiques, but it is the photos that best evoke the past, such as Stranahan trading alligator hides, otter pelts, and egret plumes with the local Seminoles. Such prizes were brought in from the Everglades in dugout canoes.
🅢 *335 SE 6th Ave., near Las Olas* • *Map D3* • *954-524-4736*

Top 10 Historical Movers and Shapers

1 William Brickell
One of the first men to take advantage of the Homestead Act of 1862.

2 Henry M. Flagler
The legal mastermind (1830–1913) who opened up Florida through railroads and luxury construction.

3 Governor Napoleon Bonaparte Broward
Elected in 1905, he enacted Florida's first conservation laws and also a program for draining the Everglades.

4 Carl Fisher
An energetic developer in the early 1900s, Fisher was the first visionary owner of Miami Beach.

5 George Merrick
The imaginative mind behind the development of Coral Gables *(see pp18–19)*.

6 The Deering Brothers
James and Charles built homes that are now major attractions *(see pp16–17 & 107)*.

7 Marjory Stoneman Douglas
The first of Florida's environmentalists, who single-handedly saved the Everglades. She died in 1998, at the age of 108.

8 Barbara Capitman
The driving force behind the movement to save the Art Deco hotels *(see p13)*.

9 Julia Tuttle
The dynamic pioneer who convinced Henry Flagler to extend his railroad down to Miami, in 1896.

10 Chief Jim Billie
Controversial Seminole chief who brought wealth to his tribe in the 1980s, by building casinos on reservations.

Left **Deco Detail** Center **Fontainebleau Hotel** Right **Mural from The Society of the Four Arts**

🔟 Architectural Wonders

1 Deco District
A national treasure of uplifting architecture. In saving it, South Miami Beach not only transformed itself but also inspired a national movement to preserve historic structures *(see pp10–13)*.

2 Biltmore Hotel and Coral Gables Congregational Church
Facing each other across lush, manicured gardens, these two structures are the heart of George Merrick's contribution to "The City Beautiful" *(see pp99 & 103)*.

3 Freedom Tower
Inspired by the famous belfry (formerly, under the Moors, a minaret for a mosque) of Seville's vast Cathedral. Sadly, the tower now stands empty *(see p83)*.

Biltmore Hotel

Ingraham insignia

4 Granada Gate
A George Merrick fantasy, with references to Spanish-Moorish architecture, in this case nodding to the Alhambra in the Iberian mountain town of Granada. ⊗ *Granada Blvd at the north entrance to Coral Gables*

5 Ingraham Building
This Renaissance-Revival beauty is a don't-miss landmark in Downtown Miami, and it evokes all the glamour of the 1920s' boom era *(see p85)*.

6 NationsBank Tower, International Place
I. M. Pei's striking take on the ziggurat theme so often used in Art Deco, looking for all the world like a stepped stack of CDs in various sizes. It's especially appealing at night when it's lit up with vibrant colors *(see p84)*.

7 Atlantis Condominium
Built by Arquitectonica in 1982 and soon thereafter one of the stars of *Miami Vice*, this "building with the hole in it" is in danger of being overrun by the rampant construction going on all along Brickell. The "hole" is an ingenious 37-ft (11-m) cube cut out of the building's center, at the 12th floor. A red spiral staircase and a palm tree draw your attention to it in a delightful way. ⊗ *2025 Brickell Ave, Miami*

Freedom Tower

8 Estefan Enterprises

Also by Arquitectonica, this playful building takes the frivolity of Deco several steps further. A free-form green-wave tower slices through a cool blue cube, at once evoking both sea and sky, while colorful dancing flotsam seem to inhabit the green wave. The roof is an oasis, with sprouting trees. *420 Jefferson Ave, Miami Beach*

9 Plymouth Congregational Church

This beautiful Mission-style edifice was built in 1916, though its massive door did come from a 17th-century monastery in the Pyrenees. *3400 Devon Road, at Main Highway, Coconut Grove*

10 Key West Old Town

Key West *(see pp26–7)* has the largest collection of 19th-century structures in the US. About 4,000 buildings, mostly houses, embody the distinctive local style. Many architectural features take their cues from elements used on ships, such as roof hatches to allow air circulation. One unique innovation is the "eyebrow" house, with second-floor windows hidden under a front porch roof overhang, providing shade in the unremitting heat.

Top 10 Murals and Mosaics

1 Fontainebleau Hotel Trompe L'oeil
A startling trompe l'oeil of a massive break in the wall graces this famous hotel *(see p148)*.

2 The Netherland
Fantastic mural of indolent sunbathers. *1330 Ocean Drive, South Beach*

3 Bacardi Import Headquarters
You can't miss the tropical foliage mosaic. Be sure to notice the building next to it, too. *2100 Biscayne Blvd*

4 Miami Beach Post Office
The classy Deco entrance has a triptych mural of Ponce de Leon and the Native American peoples. *1300 Washington Ave, South Beach*

5 Coral Gables City Hall
Denman Fink created the mural on the bell tower. The one above the stairs is by John St. John. *405 Biltmore Way*

6 Little Havana
A series of seven quirky murals. *Calle Ocho 1507–13*

7 Office Building
A 1940s mural depicting labor, the arts, and the Universe. *1617 Drexel Ave, South Beach*

8 The Society of the Four Arts
Allegorical murals from 1939. *Four Arts Plaza, Palm Beach*

9 Wyland Whaling Walls
An undersea world of whales and other cetaceans. *201 William St, Key West*

10 Bahama Village
Charming mural evoking the simplicity and beauty of Caribbean life. *Thomas St at Petronia St*

Left **Coral Castle** Center **Botánica sign** Right **Perky's Bat Tower**

Offbeat Places

1 Coral Castle

A lovesick Latvian immigrant's valentine to the girl back home who spurned him. These bizarre monoliths form one of the area's oddest monuments, yet it is strangely touching nevertheless *(see p44)*.

2 Alhambra Water Tower, Coral Gables

Alhambra Water Tower

Resembling a plump lighthouse, this colorful tower (built 1924) was the work of Denman Fink, George Merrick's uncle. Neglected for decades, it was fully restored in 1993 and, although no longer used, the tower's elegant Moorish touches make it an intriguing piece of industrial architecture. ◎ *Alhambra Circle, at Ferdinand St and Greenway Ct*

3 Ermita de la Caridad Church, Coconut Grove

Built in 1966 on the edge of Biscayne Bay, this peculiar conical church draws in Miami's Cuban exiles. The altar is oriented toward Cuba, rather than to the east, and above it is a mural depicting the history of the Catholic Church in Cuba. The shrine is dedicated to the Virgin of Charity, the Cuban patron saint. ◎ *3609 S Miami Ave, Coconut Grove*

4 Opa-Locka

Another delightful example of the quirky fantasy architecture dreamed up in the 1920s. Unfortunately, the run-down area around is anything but a dream *(see p45)*.

5 South Beach Lifeguard Huts

In all the world, it is unlikely that you'll find any lifeguard huts so aesthetically pleasing as these Deco-style delights *(see p11)*.

6 Santería and Vodou Botánicas

South Florida at its most darkly exotic. The botánicas (shops) carry all sorts of magic potions and power objects used in the practice of the hybrid religions of Santería and Vodou (voodoo) – a little Roman Catholicism mixed with a lot of ancient West African ritual and belief *(see p15)*.

Ermita de la Caridad Church

South Beach lifeguard hut

7 Stiltsville, Key Biscayne

Drive to the southernmost tip of Key Biscayne, look way out on the water, and you'll spy six lonesome structures built on stilts. These fishermen's bungalows are the last of what was once quite a community. Their number has dwindled considerably due to hurricanes and legal squabbles. *Map H4*

8 Perky's Bat Tower, Sugarloaf Key

In 1929 one Richter C. Perky, a property speculator, built this awkward structure, designed to be every bat's dream-home; in exchange, the bats were supposed to rid the area of its voracious mosquitoes. Unfortunately, the bats he imported instantly flew away, while the mosquitoes thrived. *MM 17, nr Sugarloaf Lodge*

9 Nancy's Secret Garden, Key West

Imagine entering a timeless world, full of humor and a funky, indefinable Key West aura *(see p37)*.

10 "The Garden of Eden," Key West

Devoted nudists can find an appreciative milieu in this bar *(see p124)*, as they can within the walls and gardens of many guesthouses around town. *The Bull, third floor 224 Duval St, Key West*

Top 10 Scandals

1 Barbara Meller-Jensen, Hapless Tourist
The unwary German visitor was murdered in 1993, tarnishing Miami's tourism image.

2 Laroche, Orchid Thief
In 1997, Laroche was fined for poaching with the aid of Native American Seminoles, who are exempt from the law.

3 Versace's Murder
Andrew Cunanan shot the fashion magnate on his front steps on July 15, 1997.

4 Mrs. Jeb Bush
The Florida governor's wife was caught with $19,000 of undeclared couture in 1999.

5 Elián González Standoff
The repatriation of a Cuban boy at gunpoint by the US Justice Dept hit the world's media in 2000 and tore the Cuban community here apart.

6 Presidential Election Debacle
Florida became the epicenter of the election in 2000, with the result anything but clear.

7 Estefan Lawsuits
In 2001, Cubana singer Gloria Estefan was rocked by a claim that her husband, Emilio, had sexually harassed another man.

8 Miss Cleo, TV-Telephone Psychic
2002 saw the collapse of the psychic hotline that didn't employ "genuine" psychics.

9 Bishop O'Connell's Fall from Grace
Casualty of a "topical storm" over pedophilia in 2002.

10 Rosie O'Donnell
In 2002, the talk-show hostess came out as a lesbian and championed gay adoptions in the only state to ban them.

Left **Lincoln Road Mall** Center **Hollywood Broadwalk** Right **Van Dyke Café**

Spots for People-Watching

1 Ocean Drive
The epitome of the "American Riviera." Sit in a café, or cruise up and down the strip in a convertible, on skates, or simply on foot. And, of course, if you've got it – the buff bod, golden tan, and all – Ocean Drive is the place to show it off *(see p8)*.

Ocean Drive

2 CocoWalk
A host of select shops, restaurants, outdoor cafés, and a cineplex provides the entertainment. But, here in the heart of the Grove, it's great just to hang out and listen to the live band playing most of the time on the balcony above *(see p100)*.

3 Bayside Marketplace
Never a dull moment in Downtown Miami's hottest daytime spot, featuring boutiques, live music, street performers, and ethnic dining right on the marina *(see p83)*.

4 Lincoln Road Mall
Second only to Ocean Drive in its star-quality appeal. Lined with sculpture-fountains and plants, this pedestrian area with its outdoor eateries is always lively. Score, at No. 727, is very good after dark *(see p57)*.

5 Casa Salsa
Ricky Martin's Latino-flavored club opened in 1998, featuring Puerto Rican-Spanish cuisine and cha-cha, samba, salsa, and mambo till dawn. Very easy-on-the-eye and an elegant clientele *(see p78)*.

6 Clevelander
This hotel's daytime beachfront cafés evolve into one of SoBe's top pool-bar scenes after dark. Its proximity to the beach inspires a more casual style than the usual nightspots, and there's always a crowd to enjoy happy hour and live music *(see p78)*.

7 The Forge
A 70-year institution and a perennial favorite with celebrities such as Madonna and Michael Jordan. There are atmospheric themed rooms, such as the Library, and the overall mood is cozy and

Coco Walk

romantic. The menu favors old-fashioned staples, like steaks and chocolate soufflé, and there's a

Clevelander

formidable wine cellar. ✆ *432 Arthur Godfrey Rd (41st St), Miami Beach • 305-538-8533 • \$\$\$*

8 Commodore Plaza
Coconut Grove's second most frequented spot is this intersection, where every corner features a top viewing position for the constant circulation of pedestrian traffic, everyone scoping out a café or restaurant, and each other. Try the Green Street Café *(see p102)*.

9 Hollywood Broadwalk
A rare swath of beach where a 2.5-mile (4-km) pedestrian walkway fronts directly on the sand, just to the north of Miami Beach. It's non-stop surfside fun all the way, with loads of revelers of all kinds cruising up and down *(see p24)*.

10 Mallory Square, Key West
Especially at sunset, this huge square at the Gulf end of Duval Street is a gathering place for all sorts of locals and visitors. Street performers keep it lively, and there are plenty of vendors of food and souvenirs *(see p26)*.

Sunset at Mallory Sqaure

Top 10 Trendy Cafés

1 News Café
Justifiably SoBe's most famous café *(see p8)*.

2 Van Dyke Café
Lincoln Road's top draw, both day and night, including a wraparound balcony and a jazz club *(see p78)*.

3 Green Street Café
Coconut Grove's numero uno for people-watching, happy hour, and creative meals *(see p102)*.

4 Joffrey's Coffee Co.
A choice corner spot, on Euclid, with plenty of tables outside, great coffees, and delectable pastries. ✆ *660 Lincoln Rd, S Beach*

5 Paninoteca
A wonderful place to sit and sip a drink, or to enjoy a superb pizza or salad you're invited to design yourself. ✆ *809 Lincoln Rd, S Beach & 264 Miracle Mile, Coral Gables*

6 Mango's Tropical Café
One of the hottest action venues on South Beach – live music and dancing, Floribbean dishes, and free-flowing cocktails *(see p78)*.

7 The Clay Hotel
This beautiful period building is now a youth hostel, so its modest café is always thronged with international youth *(see p152)*.

8 Books and Books
Don't let the quietness deceive you, this is a very happening place *(see p104)*.

9 11th Street Diner
One of the most popular eateries, especially with the gay crowd *(see p79)*.

10 Mangoes, Key West
A restaurant, bar, and sidewalk café, located on a busy corner *(see p125)*.

Left **The beach at 12th Street, SoBe** Right **Cathode Ray, Fort Lauderdale**

Gay and Lesbian Venues

1 Beach at 12th Street, SoBe

While all of South Beach is a gay haven, this particular stretch is where the guys tend to gather in their imposing, thong-clad throngs. ◎ Map S3–4

2 Haulover Park Beach, Miami Beach

Transvestites

Keep walking north, past the straight nude beach, and you'll soon reach the gay section – where no heavy action is tolerated. ◎ Map H3

3 Fort Lauderdale Gay Beaches

There are two major beaches "Where the Boys Are" in the Fort Lauderdale area: the stretch where Sebastian Street meets A1A; and John U. Lloyd State Park Beach. You'll know you've reached them when you sight guys with pumped muscles and skimpy swimsuits. ◎ Map D3

4 Gay and Lesbian Community Center, Fort Lauderdale

Located in very gay Wilton Manors, this is a big and well-maintained center. There's an extensive library of gay literature and reference works, friendly staff, a full calendar of special events, and plenty of opportunities for lively social interaction.
◎ 717 N Andrews Ave • 954-463-9005

5 Cathode Ray, Fort Lauderdale

This is the place to be in downtown Fort Lauderdale, especially when all the white-collar guys show up after work to relax and unwind during happy hour (2–8pm). There's a comedy night on Mondays, and the weekend high-energy partying culminates with big-screen viewing of *Queer as Folk*. ◎ 1307 East Las Olas Blvd • 954-462-8611

6 Shoppes of Wilton Manors, Fort Lauderdale

An entire gay shopping mall! Shops here include Gay Mart, In the Pink Books, Oh What a Basket, Greetings from the Rainbow, Inside Out Boutique, and Wicked Leather. There are also many prominent bars, gyms, clubs, and restaurants, such as Around the World Pizza, Chardees, and Simply Delish. ◎ 2200 block of Wilton Drive

7 Georgie's Alibi, Fort Lauderdale

This is a video bar, café, and sports bar, located in Fort Lah-Dee-Dah's unique gay shopping center, in its unique gay town – Wilton Manors – which even has its own gay mayor. The Alibi opened in April of 1997 in a then rundown area, but Wilton Manors has since blossomed into a thriving gay

The best of SoBe's gay and lesbian venues are on **p76**

Wilton Manors, Fort Lauderdale

community, and this bar has flourished with it. In fact, the Alibi is one of South Florida's best gay venues, and always worth checking out. ✆ *2266 Wilton Drive, Wilton Manors • 954-565-2526* • *www.georgiesalibi.com*

8 Coliseum, Fort Lauderdale

A newer incarnation of a former straight venue, this place is fresh and youthful, featuring lavish drag acts and an abundance of beautiful young musclemen. Every night some of the area's better-known DJs launch global groove house music "dance-a-thongs". ✆ *2520 S Miami Road • 954-832-0100 • www.coliseumnightclub.com*

9 Copa, Fort Lauderdale

One of the older gay dance clubs in town. Operating for almost 30 years, this place still packs 'em in – with drag shows, "Battle of the Bulge" and "Bare Buns" contests, and gorgeous go-go boys. It also offers video, indoor and outdoor bars, a games room, food, and cutting-edge sound and lights. As elsewhere, things really only get shaking at around midnight. ✆ *2800 S Federal Highway (Hwy 1) • 954-463-1507* • *www.copaboy.com*

10 Gay and Lesbian Community Center, Key West

Set on an appealing square, the center offers a library, a lounge, and all the information you might need. Pluses include a monthly calendar of special events, such as wine-and-cheese parties, discussion groups, and a film series. Free anonymous HIV testing is available, or just stop by for a chat. ✆ *Map A6 • 1075 Duval St, Duval Square C-14 • 305-292-3223* • *www.glcckeywest.org*

Beach at Fort Lauderdale

For exclusively gay and lesbian accommodations **See p153**

Left **Worth Avenue** Right **Collins and 7th Street, SoBe**

Aventura Mall

TOP 10 Chic Shopping Centers

1 Bal Harbour Shops

The ultimate in chi-chi, down to the English spelling of "Harbour" *(see p92)*. Here are Hermès, Gucci, Armani, Dior, Bulgari, Tiffany, Versace, and Louis Vuitton, not to mention Chanel, Dolce & Gabbana, Prada, and Lalique. Need we say more? Well, okay, Nieman Marcus, and Saks Fifth Avenue. ◈ *9700 Collins Avenue • Map H2 • 954-760-4005 • www.balharbourshops.com*

Gucci emblem

2 Village of Merrick Park

The brand-new Village of Merrick Park offers luxury retail stores, set amid an immaculate urban garden ideal for concerts. Neiman Marcus and Miami's very first Nordstrom are at its heart, along with a range of fine shops and places to eat, such as the elegant Palm Restaurant. The Mediterranean-Revival style, with landscaped walkways and fountains, is in keeping with the precedent set by the city's founder George Merrick *(see pp18–19)*. ◈ *Miracle Mile, Coral Gables*

3 Collins and 7th Street, SoBe

For your upscale shopping convenience, all the SoBe boutiques that seriously matter are clustered around this intersection. ◈ *Map R4*

4 The Falls

Semi-open-air arcades with waterfalls and tropical vegetation form the backdrop to over 100 shops. Mostly upscale, they include Bloomingdale's, Macy's, Banana Republic, the Pottery Barn, and the Discovery Channel Store for kids. In addition, there are 12 movie screens and some 13 restaurants and cafés, including the inevitable Haagen Däzs and Mrs. Field's Cookies. ◈ *8888 SW 136th St. • 305-255-4570 • www.shopthefalls.com*

5 Aventura Mall

Lord & Taylor, Bloomingdale's, Burdines, and Macy's are the upscale anchors, in addition to specialty stores including Abercrombie & Fitch, Ann Taylor, Guess?, J. Crew, FAO Schwarz, Fossil, and Clinique. Art galleries, some

Boca Raton

excellent restaurants, an international food court, and a 24-screen cineplex complete the picture. Biscayne Blvd & 196th St, Aventura • 305-935-1110 • www.shop aventuramall.com

6 Dadeland Mall
Fear not! There is a Saks Fifth Avenue even way down in South Miami – plus some 170 high-end specialty shops and several other fine anchor stores, including Florida's largest Burdine's. Unless you're shopping on the cheap, just ignore the fact that there's also a JC Penney, a Radio Shack, and a Best Buy. The décor is pleasing, if a bit predictable – palm-tree pillars and ceilings painted to resemble skies. ❧ 7535 N Kendall Drive • 305-665-6226

7 Worth Avenue, Palm Beach
Loads of marvelously expensive, ultra-exclusive must-haves for the crème of the haves (see p25).

8 Las Olas Boulevard and the Galleria
Fort Lauderdale's high-end shopping is spread between its main street downtown and a mall just near the beach. Las Olas' 100-plus boutiques are unique, all mixed with some really good restaurants. The Galleria, East Sunrise Blvd at A1A, offers Neiman Marcus, Saks Fifth Avenue, and Lord & Taylor.

9 Boca Raton
Newly expanded, Boca's premier mall just took a quantum leap into even greater luxury. It now has a Nordstrom to go with its Saks, Cartier, Tiffany, Lord & Taylor, Bloomie's, and Williams-Sonoma. Set amid exotic foliage, skylights, hand-glazed tiles, and sculptural accents, there's also a fancy cuisine court – no fast-food chain joints here! If you venture into downtown Boca, be sure to stroll through pastel-pink Mizner Park, where you'll also find more chic shopping options. ❧ Town Center 6000 W Glades Road • 561-368-6000

10 Duval Street, Key West
Besides the tacky T-shirt shops, Key West's main drag (see p26) is also home to some superb emporiums of quality merchandise, including: clothing at Fast Buck Freddie's (No. 500); Sunlion Jewelry (No. 513); Island Furniture and Accessories (No. 1024); Gingerbread Square Gallery, mixing local artists and world-class glass blowers (No. 1207); and Archeo Ancient Art, which specializes in African art and Persian rugs (No. 1208).

Miami's Top 10

Left **Ceramic Art Deco buildings** Center **South Beach boutique** Right **Española Way**

TOP 10 Malls and Markets

Bayside Marketplace

1 Bayside Marketplace
This sprawling marketplace abounds with chain boutiques, the occasional trendy local shop adding spice. *(see p83)*.

2 Sawgrass Mills Mall
This claims to be the largest shopping center in the world, a boast you'll believe as you drive its circumference trying to find the way in. This 8-acre (3-ha) mercantile behemoth comprises more than 300 discount outlets, from top-of-the-line goods to bargain basement rejects.
Ⓢ *12801 W Sunrise Blvd, at Flamingo Rd*
• *1-800-356-4557*

3 Seybold Building
Located just off Flagler Street, where all sorts of cut-rate electronics can be haggled

over, this building specializes in gems and jewelry, both wholesale and retail. Mainly a place for jewelers to pick up stock, ordinary mortals, too, can rummage the sparklers and invest in either loose gems or unique pieces of fine jewelry. Ⓢ *36 NE 1st St*
• *305-374-7922*

4 Dolphin Mall
More than 200 stores fill Greater Miami's newest middle-range mall. In part, this is an outlet for such heavy hitters as Saks Fifth Avenue, Brooks Brothers, Giorgio's et al., but there is also a host of boutiques as well as a 19-screen cineplex at the heart of it all, on the "Ramblas", where the liveliest eateries are found.
Ⓢ *11401 NW 12th Street* • *305-365-7446*
• *www.shopdolphinmall.com*

5 Dania Beach Historic Antiques District
Here is South Florida's largest concentration of antiques shops. More than 100 dealers offer an array of furniture, fine art, and jewelry, as well as glass, pottery and china, and various other collectibles. Prices vary greatly, so shop around for bargains.
Ⓢ *Federal Highway 1 north for two blocks from Dania Beach Blvd*

Dolphin Mall

Antiques District

6 Española Way Market

On Saturday and Sunday, there's a small, rather esoteric market along here, selling flowers, arts and crafts, and organic products. An array of vaguely hippie items also make an appearance, such as amulets, scented candles, stones, oriental bric-a-brac, and exotic clothing – all natural, of course. You can get your palm read, too, or decorated with henna if you prefer. ⑤ *15th St, South Beach • Map R3*

7 Los Pinareños Fruteria

Little Havana's foremost fruit and veg market, and you can get fresh juice, snacks, and flowers, too *(see p88)*.

8 Opa-Locka/Hialeah Flea Market

Up to 1,200 dealers show up here seven days a week from 7am–7pm, hawking everything and anything you can think of to satisfy an orgy of acquisition. Weekends are best, when the number of dealers, browsers, and bargain-hunters swells. ⑤ *12705 NW 47th Ave*

9 Lincoln Road Markets

This lively pedestrian area, graced with attractive fountains and upscale restaurants and shops, also offers various markets. On Sunday, there's one selling fruit and flowers, plus regional products, and specialties. Every other Sunday from October to May, there's also a collectors' market, and on the second Tuesday of the month "Arts on the Road" features all sorts of work. ⑤ *Lincoln Road, between Washington Ave and Alton Rd • Map Q–R2*

10 The Swap Shop

Eighty-eight acres (35 ha) of shopping at bargain prices. The outdoor flea market features antiques, collectibles, clothing, plants, and a farmers' market. Inside, in addition to an international food court and a video arcade, there's a huge entertainment center with a show Wed–Mon put on by the Hanneford Family Circus, complete with elephants! The complex also claims the world's largest drive-in theater. ⑤ *3291 W Sunrise Blvd, between I-95 & Florida's Turnpike, Fort Lauderdale • www.floridaswapshop.com*

Lincoln Road market

Left **Lola** Center **Jazid** Right **Liquid dance floor**

🔟 Nightlife

crobar

1 crobar
Housed in an architectural gem, the former Cameo Theater, this is high-tech fun at its most cutting-edge. crobar is glitzy and full of attitude, and you should definitely wear your Prada bowling shoes, or whatever's the latest thing to turn the fashion cognoscenti's heads *(see p77)*.

2 Jazid
A special place in Miami Beach for those who appreciate jazz. South Florida's top musicians perform nightly. Since there's no cover, do the right thing and order a drink or two to make sure this haven of anti-chic stays afloat. You're there for the music, the real thing in a sea of glamorous SoBe hype *(see p77)*.

3 Lola
An understated choice favored by locals, where you can hear yourself think, and your friends talk! Neither edgy nor elegant, but regulars praise it for its "reality factor." A cozy gathering place for friends up for slightly subdued fun *(see p77)*.

4 B.E.D.
Mixed gay and straight clientele, famous food, and, yes, beds, and only beds, for dining on or for flopping when you take a break from bopping. Gimmicky it may be, but devotees say it's "just the right mix of weird and wonderful" *(see p77)*.

5 Opium Garden
Where you could very well rub elbows with a celebrity or two, if you can get in. At its peak of recherché cachet at the time of writing, it's popularity with the big-name stars is bound to wane, but one visit will confirm its undeniable charms *(see p77)*.

6 Rumi
For the neo-lounge-lizard-mystic in you, trance and world music is a specialty. The medieval Islamic poet for whom it is named would probably never fathom Rumi's allure, but regulars swear it's the only place in SoBe with "spiritual" dimension *(see p77)*.

Rumi

South Beach is the focus of Miami's nightlife. For nightlife in the Keys See pp123–4

Liquid

Top 10 Tropical Tipples

1 Mojito
Papa Hemingway's favorite splash: light rum, crushed mint leaves, sugar, and lime to taste. Sublime!

2 Hurricane
For a howling success, mix dark and light rums, blue Curaçao, and lemon juice.

3 Piña Colada
The blend of coconut milk, pineapple juice, and a choice rum is impossible to beat.

4 Rum Runner
Shades of Prohibition-era Caribbean smugglers, this classic comes in many styles and fruity flavors: watermelon, grenadine, blackberry, etc.

5 Sangria
The variations of fruit in red wine are almost endless.

6 Cosmopolitan
Variations on this vodka and Cointreau theme are creative. Often done with cranberry and/or orange notes.

7 Daiquiri
Another timeless Caribbean rum concoction, any way you like it: mango, strawberry, lime, peach, guava, etc.

8 Margarita
Not neglecting this south-of-the-border treat, in regular and frozen incarnations, paired with any fruit – and a range of liqueurs, too.

9 Mai Tai
One version of the Polynesian perennial features crème de noyaux, banana, grenadine, and tropical juices.

10 Martini
Be prepared for this old standby to appear in a thousand creative guises: with unexpected fruit liqueurs, for example, or even with white or milk chocolate!

7 Liquid
A hyper-technological affair; very popular and it may be difficult to get past the velvet rope. Two music rooms feature the area's top DJs. Although it's part of a national chain, the place appeals to a "hipper" clientele, who dig its "underground" mystique (see p77).

8 Billboardlive
A little bit for everyone here – sometimes gay, sometimes straight – offering DJs, live bands, tea dances, and special events. Fast becoming one of the new SoBe institutions (see p77).

9 Twist
SoBe's premier gay venue, huge and always jumping, but it doesn't get started until very late, of course, and then it goes till dawn. Don't show before midnight unless you want to be considered a desperate wallflower. So popular of late that even straight people are beginning to take to it (see p76).

10 Rise (formerly Salvation and 1771)
Despite the name confusion, there's no gender confusion here, at one of Miami's top gay spots. Note the address, 1771 West Avenue, because whatever this joint ends up being called next, the location will endure (see p76).

Left **Stone crab claws** Right **Tap Tap**

🔟 Restaurants

Norman's, Coral Gables

inventiveness without limits are the keynotes here, taste-bud awakening combinations of Oriental and local ingredients that will have you marveling at the chef's ingenuity *(see p79)*.

1 Norman's, Coral Gables
Haute-nouvelle-evolved fusion cuisine at its peak of foodie perfection. Norman has gained a much-deserved national and international reputation for his subtle inventiveness, and he's published a number of books revealing some, but not all, of his secrets *(see p105)*.

2 Mark's South Beach, South Beach
Another connoisseur's dream spot, just a block from the chicest beach in the US, at the Post-Modernized Hotel Nash. The setting is dreamy, to go with the artfully presented food *(see p79)*.

3 Pacific Time, South Beach
Lincoln Road's answer to fusion sublimity. Freshness and

4 Escopazzo, South Beach
As close to authentic Italian food as you're likely to get outside of the peninsula itself. It's more or less family style, so you'll feel like one of the regulars in this unpretentious little place *(see p79)*.

5 Tap Tap, South Beach
Colors and more colors greet the eye everywhere you look, most of it semi-religious imagery depicting various beneficent Voodoo gods and goddesses. Hearty, simple – and spicy – Haitian flavors stimulate the palate *(see p79)*.

6 Versailles, Little Havana
Everybody's favorite Cuban restaurant is an essential stop on a visit to Little Havana – a busy,

Left **Mark's South Beach** Right **Tap Tap interior**

Joe's Stone Crab

fairly rambunctious place. Cuban food tends to be a challenge to delicate digestive systems, but it's authentic *(see pp15 & 89)*.

7 Joe's Stone Crab, South Beach

A SoBe institution and always packed, despite being vast. Located right on the beach, it's always lots of fun and consistently excellent, although a bit too touristy for some *(see p79)*.

8 Café Tu Tu Tango, Coconut Grove

A friendly, engaging theme restaurant – real artists paint while you dine – that turns out light, nouvelle Floribbean food. Located in the Grove's groovy downtown CocoWalk complex, it's always bustling with good-looking 20- and 30-somethings *(see p105)*.

9 Monty's Stone Crab Seafood House and Raw Bar, Coconut Grove

Order a pile of peel-and-eat shrimp and a dollop or two of cocktail sauce, and seat yourself under a thatched breezeway while you shuck. Right on the water, near Coconut Grove's parks, it's one of the nicest places to have a casual meal *(see p105)*.

10 Cancun Grill, Miami Lakes

Exceptional Mexican cuisine at reasonable prices. This is the real thing, unpretentious and full of local color *(see p89)*.

Top 10 Floribbean Food and Drink

1 Café Cubano (Cafecito)
A tiny cup of intensely sweet, black coffee is the mainstay of life for many. If you want it with a drop of milk, ask for a *cortadito*.

2 Conch Chowder or Fritters
The snail- or slug-like creature that lives in beautiful pink shells is served up in a traditional, rather chewy dish.

3 Black Beans and Rice
"Moors and Christians" is the staple of the Cuban diet. Its savory, smoky flavor complements almost everything.

4 Yucca/Plantain Chips
The variations on bananas and potatoes are often served as deep-fried chips – slightly sweet and aromatic.

5 Blackened Grouper
Having your fish cooked "blackened" is a Cajun recipe that has caught on in most restaurants in South Florida.

6 Ceviche
A seafood marinade using lime juice, onions, green bell peppers, and cilantro (coriander).

7 Lechon Asado
Pork is a big part of the Cuban diet. This term translates as "roast suckling pig," and is the ultimate feast.

8 Chimichurri
A sauce with olive oil, garlic, lemon juice or wine vinegar, and parsley. Jalapeño peppers are optional.

9 Key Lime Pie
The Key lime looks more like a lemon but makes the most exquisite pie.

10 Alfajores
A typical Cuban pastry composed of chocolate, custard, and coconut.

For more great places to eat in Miami and the Keys
See pp79, 89, 95, 105, 111, 125 & 130

Left **Lifeguard hut on the Gold Coast** Center **Deco District** Right **Little Haiti, reached on Hwy 1**

TOP 10 Drives and Walks

Downtown Miami

1 Miami Beach to Tip of Key Biscayne

From South Beach, drive west on 5th Street, which becomes the MacArthur Causeway, I-395. Great views to be had over the water and the posh artificial islands, notably Star, Palm, and Hibiscus. Soon you'll be soaring over Downtown on the overpass that leads around to I-95, getting a bird's-eye view of the many skyscrapers, which are particularly attractive at night. Just before I-95 ends, take the exit for Key Biscayne. Stop at the Rickenbacker Causeway tollbooth ($1). The high arching road offers more great views of the skyline and takes you to deserted Virginia Key and then to quiet Key Biscayne. ✤ Map H3–4

2 Routes North

There are three ways to make your way by car north from Miami: Interstate 95 is the fastest, unless it's rush hour, but is really only to be used if you have a certain destination in mind. Highway 1 is closer to the sea, but is lined with local businesses practically all the way, so the stop-and-go traffic can be a real drag. A1A, however, makes the time spent decidedly worthwhile, rewarding the traveler with a range of natural beauty and elegant neighborhoods of the Gold and Treasure Coasts *(see pp24–5 & 128).*

3 Miami to Key West

You can do this drive in about three-and-a-half hours, but why hurry? There are great sights along the way, like the fantastic giant lobster at Treasure Village artists' colony. It's also definitely worth a stop to have a great seafood lunch or dinner on the water. Other attractions include parks and nature preserves *(see pp36–7),* and Perky's Bat Tower *(see p49).* ✤ Map D4–A6

The Everglades

Tips for getting around Miami are on **p137**

SoBe hotels

4 Everglades Trails

There are several roads for exploring the Everglades: I-75, Alligator Alley; Hwy 41, the Tamiami Trail; or the less developed road (No. 9336) from Florida City. Off all of these roads, you'll find many opportunities for excursions into the wild *(see also pp28–9 & 127)*.

5 Deco District

With some 800 Tropical Deco wonders to behold, you can hardly miss; just walk or bike along Ocean Drive, and Collins and Washington Avenues between about 5th and 22nd Streets *(see also pp10–13)*.
Ⓢ Map R5–S1

6 SoBe Streetlife

Almost synonymous with the Deco District. All the action is concentrated in three areas: Ocean Drive and the parallel streets of Collins and Washington (where most of the clubs are); the seductive Lincoln Road and the Española Way pedestrian malls *(see also pp8–9 & 57)*.

7 Calle Ocho

The main walking part of Little Havana lies along SW 8th Street, between about 11th and 17th Avenues. But interesting spots are quite spread out for blocks around, and most of them are best found by driving, then exploring on foot *(see pp14–15)*.

8 Coco Village

Always lively, usually with young, perky people, this is downtown Coconut Grove. As well as shops, outdoor eateries, and cafés, live bands often play in CocoWalk *(see also pp98–105)*.

9 Key West Old Town

The only sensible way to get around Key West is either on foot or by bike; there's so much detail to take in and, besides, parking is usually a problem here. A planned tour can be fine *(see p121)*, but it's just as good to walk wherever inspiration leads *(see also pp26–7)*.

10 Palm Beach

To experience the essence of this wealthy community, begin your walk at Worth Ave. on the beach at Ocean Blvd. Walk west and check out as many of the fabulous shops as you dare. Continue on to Addison Mizner's pink palace, Casa de Leoni (No. 450), then take Lake Drive north to Royal Palm Way. Visit the Society of the Four Arts, then continue on north to the Flagler Museum. Finally, go east along Royal Poinciana Way and south to The Breakers *(see p25)*.

Mallory Square, Key West

Left **Fairchild Tropical Garden** Right **Hotel Place St. Michel**

🔟 Romantic Spots

1 Villa Vizcaya Gardens
A glorious pastiche of styles from more or less 500 years of European architecture, most of it bought in the Old World by an early 20th-century farm machinery magnate to be remodeled into this comfortable palace *(see pp16–17)*.

2 Venetian Pool
A lush fantasy of water, gardens, and sculpted stone, where Esther Williams (bathing-beauty diva of yesteryear) used to star in synchronized swimming movies. The pool was born of the mind of visionary entrepreneur George Merrick *(see pp18–19)*.

3 Ancient Spanish Monastery Cloister and Gardens
With its magnificent gardens and cloisters redolent of ancient lands and courtly love, this has become a popular spot for weddings. The building can be traced back to 12th-century Spain, though it didn't make its way to Florida

Ancient Spanish Monastery

until the 20th century. Having lain dormant in packing crates for years, it was finally reassembled in the 1950s *(see p91)*.

4 Fairchild Tropical Garden
The tranquil, silvery lakes, broad vistas and lush, dappled retreats are capable of bringing out the romantic in anyone. Badly damaged by Hurricane Andrew in 1992, the gardens have made a brilliant comeback, and are certainly worth a stroll to inhale the fragrant, shaded bowers, and perhaps stay for dinner at the nearby Red Fish Grill *(see also p107)*.

Venetian Pool

Morikami

5 Coral Castle
One Edward Leedskalnin created this huge coral rock Valentine heart to win back his fickle love. She remained unmoved by his Herculean labors, however, and he died here alone in 1951 *(see also p107)*.

6 Morikami Japanese Gardens
The 1,000-year-old originals of some of these deeply peaceful settings were designed for Japanese nobility – places of inspiration for them to recite poetry to each other, or to seek solace in troubled times. Few places evoke the serenity and spiritual depth you can sense here, in the silent rocks and the murmuring cascades *(see also p37)*.

7 Tantra
Aphrodisiac cuisine in an erotic arena evoke a sense of Indo-Persian culture. Real grass carpets and sensuous sculptures and paintings set the tone. Sublime Middle-Eastern and Indian fusion dishes are served in a somewhat desultory, yet suggestive, fashion in a candlelit ambience where palm fans softly spin. ⊗ *1445 Pennsylvania Ave • 305-672-4765 • $$$$$*

8 Red Fish Grill
Perhaps the most starry-eyed setting in Miami, with its shimmering bay views and evocatively lighted foliage. The potent backdrop of Biscayne Bay, Fairchild Tropical Gardens, and nearby Mattheson Hammock Park and saltwater Atoll Pool make this an unforgettable place to dine. Attentive service and delicious food *(see p111)*.

9 Hotel Place St. Michel
French-style boutique hotel with an exquisite restaurant. Stay a night or two and you'll think you're in a chic little pension in Paris. The subtly lit bistro is a perfect place for a quietly intimate tête-à-tête, yet all this is within walking distance of downtown Coral Gables *(see also pp105 & 150)*.

10 Mallory Square, Key West, at sunset
Although you will most likely be there with a hoard of other sunset-viewers, the beauty of this moment and the general air of merriment will provide you with a memorable experience. Watch a tall ship sail in front of the huge setting sun, blazing orangy-pink at the Gulf's edge. True romantics should keep an eye out for the beguiling green flash that's said to occur just before the sun disappears below the horizon – if you catch it, it means good luck in love *(see also p26)*.

Left **Museum of Science and Space** Right **Historical Museum of Southern Florida**

⑩ Children's Attractions

1 South Haulover Beach
One of the best and least crowded beaches, with a mix of grass and dunes to play in *(see p30)*.

2 Hobie Beach
An excellent stretch of beach, popular not only with windsurfers but also with families appreciative of its calm, shallow waters *(see pp30–31)*.

3 Miami Seaquarium
Lolita the killer whale, Flipper the movie-star dolphin, and Salty the sea lion are all on hand to thrill the kids *(see p72)*.

4 Amelia Earhart Park
A fun and wholesome day out. There's a petting zoo with lots of baby animals and pony rides on weekends. There are also

Parrots, Metrozoo

islands to search out, beaches to explore, playgrounds, and fish-filled lakes. Blacksmiths demonstrate their skills, as do other craftsmen, and the whole is delightfully uncrowded, as the park is well away from the tourist track. ◎ *401 E 65th St, at NW 42nd Ave • 305-685-8389 • 9am–5pm daily • Adm*

5 Miami Metrozoo
This zoo is an endless delight for children. At the children's petting zoo, there are regularly scheduled "Ecology Theater" presentations, where children can touch all sorts of exotic species and learn about the local Florida environment as well. Also near the entrance is Dr. Wilde's World, where, among other hands-on exhibits, you can explore "The Wonders of Tropical America."

Hobie Beach

Children are well cared for in South Florida's hotels – See p145

Other experiences include sniff stations, animal puzzles, and a sensory game wall *(see p107)*.

6 Storytelling

Every Thursday at 7pm, in the plush, beautiful lobby of the historic Biltmore Hotel in Coral Gables, it's storytelling time around the fireplace. Youngsters may also enjoy a visit to the finches in their elaborate cages, as well as a stroll around the gardens and the fountains within the grounds *(see p99)*.

7 Historical Museum of Southern Florida

The Downtown museum has created a number of hands-on activities and multimedia programs, such as an exploration of the Everglades' ecology, past and present *(see also p42)*.

8 Museum of Science and Space Transit Planetarium

The young and curious will find much to capture their attention and imagination in this multi-faceted facility. There are over 140 hands-on exhibits to explore the worlds of sound, light, and gravity, not to mention the chance to hug a dinosaur. Outside – beyond the collections of fossils, mounted insects, spiders, and butterflies – lies the Wildlife Center, home to birds, tortoises, and enormous snakes. The state-of-the-art Planetarium offers laser light shows set to rock music. ✆ 3280 S Miami Ave • Museum: 305-646-4200 • Planetarium: 305-646-4400 • www.miamisci.org • 10am–6pm daily; closed Thanksgiving & Christmas • Adm

9 Mini Amore – European Fashions for Children

If your kids are demanding designer duds, this is the top shop. Couturier masters such as

Miami Seaquarium

Moschino and Versace have begun creating trendy threads for the preschool-to-adolescent market. ✆ 3015 Grand Ave, No. 173 CocoWalk, Coconut Grove • 305-444-8440 • Sun–Thu, 11am–10pm, Fri & Sat, 11am–midnight

10 Key West Aquarium

The Touch Tank is a great attraction for children, allowing them to pick up starfish, native conchs, and horseshoe crabs. Elsewhere, they even get the chance to pet a live shark. When it opened, in 1934, this was Key West's first tourist attraction, and it continues to draw capacity crowds, not only for its hands-on features, but also for the highly entertaining and educational guided tours. Seeing the amazing and rare sawfish go to work during feeding time is not to be missed. ✆ 1 Whitehead St at Mallory Square • Map A6 • 305-296-2051 • www.keywestaquarium.com • 10am–6pm daily • Adm

AROUND MIAMI AND THE KEYS

MIAMI'S TOP 10

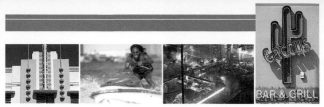

Left **Art Deco hotel** Center left **Jet skier** Center right **Liquid Night Club** Right **Cactus Bar and Grill**

Miami Beach and Key Biscayne

NOWHERE ELSE ON EARTH *seems to be so happily addicted to glamour as Miami Beach. All the traits of modern life are here, pushed to the limit: symbols of speed, wealth, and status are vaunted everywhere you look in this body-conscious, sexually charged resort. Key Biscayne, the next big island to the south, provides a stark contast to the dynamism and self-consciousness of its neighbor; here you will find a tranquil and family-oriented atmosphere pervading parks, perfect beaches, and a scattering of museums.*

Delano Hotel

Sights

1. SoBe and the Deco District
2. Parrot Jungle
3. The Wolfsonian
4. Bass Museum of Art
5. Miami Seaquarium
6. Crandon Park
7. Marjory Stoneman Douglas Biscayne Nature Center
8. Harbor Drive
9. Bill Baggs Cape Florida State Recreation Area
10. Cape Florida Lighthouse

Park Central Hotel

Cavalier Hotel, Deco District

1 SoBe and the Deco District

Posh high-life and decadent low-life meet and the fun never stops in the vibrant beach-and-nightclub community of South Beach – otherwise known as SoBe *(see pp8–9)*. The world-famous Deco District *(see pp10–13),* an essential element of Miami Beach, is beautifully preserved in hundreds of colorful, inspired buildings.

2 Parrot Jungle

Over 1,100 birds populate this beautiful tropical garden, scheduled to re-open in its new location on Watson Island in spring 2003 (until the end of 2002 it was located at 11000 SW 57th Ave, south of Coral Gables). Come face-to-face with talkative cockatoos, menacing reptiles, and bizarre insects. In the ever-popular Trained Bird Show, some of the talented feathered friends perform various tricks for you, such as riding on roller skates.

Elsewhere you can meet baby orangutans, check out different types of turtles, and, of course, come jaw-to-jaw with the ubiquitous alligators – be sure not to miss the rare albino one!
§ *Watson Island in Biscayne Bay nr the Port of Miami • www.parrotjungle.com • 305-666-7834 • 9:30am–6pm • Adm*

3 The Wolfsonian

A wonderful museum and design research institute that traces the origins of Deco and other significant modern artistic trends within this 1920s' former storage facility *(see pp22–3).*

The Wolfsonian façade

4 Bass Museum of Art

This Mayan-influenced Deco structure of the 1930s came of age in 1964, when John and Johanna Bass donated their extensive collection of art. It consists mainly of 15th–17th-century European paintings, sculpture, and textiles, and highlights include Renaissance and Baroque works, as well as paintings by Dürer and Rubens, and a 16th-century Flemish tapestry. More modern pieces include lithographs by Léger and Toulouse-Lautrec.
§ *2121 Park Ave, South Beach • Map S1 • 305-673-7530 • www.bass museum.org • 10am–5pm Tue, Thu–Sat; 11am–5pm Sun; Adm*

Ghirlandaio painting, Bass Museum

Killer whale, Miami Seaquarium

enormously wide, with palm trees and picnic areas. The waters are calm and shallow, and good for snorkeling. There are also concession stands, 75 barbecue grills, a winding boardwalk, and convenient parking. Very popular for parties. ◈ Map H3

5 Miami Seaquarium

This has been a Miami institution since the 1960s, when the hit TV series *Flipper* was filmed here. Trained dolphins still swim in the cove where Flipper once swam, and you can join them under a trainer's watchful eye for a fee. There are live shows throughout the day, featuring sea lions and killer whales as well as dolphins. Other areas provide viewing stations to see manatees, sharks, a mangrove of pelicans, and a coral reef aquarium. ◈ *4400 Rickenbacker Causeway, Virginia Key • Map H3 • 305-361-5705 • www.miami seaquarium.com • 9.30am–6pm daily; Adm*

6 Crandon Park

Key Biscayne is blessed with some of Miami's top beaches. Certainly the most impressive is this one, which is actually rated among the top ten in the country. Located on the upper half of the key, it's 3 miles (5 km) long and

Miami Vice

September 16, 1984, was a day that was to transform Miami almost overnight. It was the day *Miami Vice* debuted on TV, setting the stage for this city to conquer the world of high-profile glitz and hedonism. Suddenly the slick, cotton-candy-colored world of edgy outlaws, fast cars, and deals caught the global imagination, and Miami was the place to be.

7 Marjory Stoneman Douglas Biscayne Nature Center

Part of Crandon Park, this center contains a unique black mangrove reef of fossilized wood and roots along the northeast shore of Key Biscayne. Wearing suitable foot protection, you can wade in shallow waters to explore the underwater world. The nature center is named after the woman who almost single-handedly saved the Everglades from being overrun by housing developments, and it offers information and guided tours. ◈ *4000 Crandon Blvd, Key Biscayne • Map H4*

8 Harbor Drive

Winding along the western shore, this is the heart of Key Biscayne's upscale residential district. The lucky ones with houses on the outer side of the road have magnificent views of Downtown Miami from their back gardens. Although the area has its share of mansions, most of the houses are more modestly proportioned. Still, it's a rarefied neighborhood where flocks of ibis can be found picking away on someone's lawn. ◈ *Map G4*

9 Bill Baggs Cape Florida State Recreation Area

This beach, also rated among the nation's top ten, is conveniently joined to picnic areas and

Boardwalk, Bill Baggs

pavilions by boardwalks across the dunes. The sugary sand is sometimes marred by clumps of seaweed, but it is the stinging man-o'-war jellyfish that you need to watch out for most. ⬡ *Map H4 • 305-361-5811 • Adm*

10 Cape Florida Lighthouse
The oldest structure in South Florida has been standing sentinel since 1825. In 1836, it was destroyed by Native Americans, only to be reborn 10 years later. It has since withstood some blistering meteorological onslaughts, but the worst threat came from simple neglect following its dismissal from duties 1878. Only in 1966 did its renovation and preservation begin. ⬡ *Map H4 • Tours at 10am and 1pm; 109 steps to the top*

Cape Florida Lighthouse

A Walk Through the Deco District

Morning

🕐 From the southern end of the District on **Ocean Drive**, at 6th Street, head northward, checking out not just the façades but also as many of the hotel interiors as you can. Many have unique design elements in the lobbies, bars, and gardens.

Between the **Leslie** and the **Cardozo** is the wonderful **Carlyle**, currently undergoing a major restoration.

Turn left after the Cavalier, and go to the next street over, **Collins Avenue**. Turn right on Collins and check out **Hoffman's Cafeteria** at 1450, built in curved Nautical style in 1939 by Henry Hohauser. Stop here for lunch.

Mid-afternoon

A little farther on, you'll find the **St. Moritz Hotel**, which features a cut coral façade and neon.

At 1685, you can't miss the all-white **Delano**, with its landmark winged tower. The outlandish post-modern interiors are by Philippe Starke, and contain original Dali and Gaudi furniture.

Next stop is the **Ritz Plaza**, with another fantasy tower in glass block. When you get to 21st St, turn left; on the next corner you will encounter the **Abbey Hotel**, with its marvelous salamander motif and Flash Gordon-style towers.

A little over a block farther on is the chrome-trimmed **Governor Hotel** – and time for drinks.

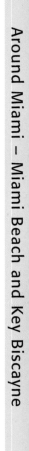

For more on the Deco District **See pp10–13**

Left **Fishing** Center **Cycling** Right **Diving**

TOP10 Sports Options

1 Swimming
The hotel pool or the surging gray-blue Atlantic Ocean? This is Florida, and swimming is number one – snorkeling, too, in quieter areas, especially Crandon Park on Key Biscayne *(see p72)* and off South Pointe.

2 Volleyball
Anywhere there's a developed beach, you'll find a volleyball net and a quorum of players. Lummus Park is the best place to show off your skills to Miami's greatest beach bums, but South Pointe Park's a close contender.

3 Fishing
Deep-sea fishing out in the ocean, or the more conventional kind off a jetty or pier – both are readily available. The jetty or Sunshine Pier at First Street Beach on Miami Beach is good, or the breaker area just south of the Lighthouse on Key Biscayne.

4 Bicycling
The best way to get around both Miami Beach and Key Biscayne. ❧ *Mangrove Cycles, 260 Crandon Blvd, Key Biscayne, 305-361-5555 • Miami Beach Bicycle Center, 601 5th Street, South Beach, 305-674-0150.*

5 Jet-skiing
At Hobie Island Beach *(see p30)* you can rent one of these exciting modes of fun on the water, or head over to Virgina Key and you'll find Jet Ski Beach, with lots of rental stands.

6 Tennis
There are plenty of tennis courts all over the islands.
❧ *Information about public courts, Miami-Dade County Parks and Recreation Department, 305-755-7800 • Flamingo Tennis Center, 1000 12th St, S Beach*

7 Golf
So that he could play golf year-round is the main reason that Jackie Gleason *(see p39)* moved to Miami. The Crandon Golf Course is one of the best.
❧ *6700 Crandon Boulevard, on Key Biscayne • 305-361-9129.*

8 Windsurfing and Surfing
For windsurfing, the intra-coastal waterways are calmer and there's almost always a breeze; check out Windsurfer Beach on Virginia Key for rentals. For surfing, the waves on the Atlantic side are plenty gnarly; the best spot is just off First Street Beach.

9 Kite-Flying
A very popular activity, given the prevailing maritime winds. There's even a park especially for kite enthusiasts at the south end of Haulover Park.

10 Workouts
South Pointe Park has a "Vita Course," a fitness circuit you can huff and puff your way through while taking in the views of the port, and enjoying the relative spaciousness compared to the crowds of Lummus Park.

For more about sports activities in South Florida
See pp34–5

Left **SoBe shops** Right **Morgan on Collins Avenue**

🔟 Shopping

1 Collins Avenue at 7th Street, South Beach
The block or two around this intersection has all the designer boutiques you'll ever need, from Versace Jeans Couture to Club Monaco, with its carefully selected knockoffs. Also check out the side-street stores. ◈ Map R4

2 DD of Ocean Drive
Situated in the heart of the action is a boutique of SoBe style, haute hip club-gear for the fashionably proactive of both sexes. ◈ 924 Ocean Drive

3 South Beach News and Tobacco
A convenience store, but the stars are the cigars, either hand-rolled on the premises or imported from everywhere but Cuba. ◈ 710 Washington Ave, No. 9, South Beach

4 Art Deco District Welcome Center
A treasure-trove of Deco kitsch to take home as your very own. Everything from cutesy salt-&-pepper sets to really rather nice reproduction lamps. ◈ 1001 Ocean Drive, South Beach

5 South Beach Couture
A couple of blocks off the beach and so, presumably, a bit less costly, but the names are the same: Versace, Armani, D&G, DKNY – fine clothing for men and women. Shirts start at about $85. ◈ 1201 Washington Ave

6 Kafka's Used Book Store & Cyber Café
Yes, books in the middle of South Beach, and a reference to Franz Kafka, no less. Just in case you suddenly start feeling intellectual on the beach. ◈ 1460 Washington Ave, at 14th St, South Beach

7 Esperanto Music
If your visit to Miami stimulates a taste for Latin music, this is the place to indulge it. ◈ 513 Lincoln Rd, at Drexel Ave

8 Frit's Skate Shop
Get yourself a pair of in-line skates, to rent or buy, and take some free lessons (Sunday mornings). Scooters available, too. ◈ 726 Lincoln Rd, at Euclid Ave

9 The 9th Chakra
The mystic arts are here, everything from prophecy to realignment through crystals, and feng shui – all the apparatus and books you may require. Ask what the store's name is about for a quick lesson in metaphysics. ◈ 811 Lincoln Rd, between Meridian Ave and Jefferson Ave

10 Key Biscayne
The Square Shopping Center, 260 Crandon Boulevard, and several other generic types nearby are just about all that you'll find on Key Biscayne. They contain a few art galleries, small clothing boutiques, and the usual mix of banks, chain stores, and dentists.

➔ *Miami Beach also has markets on Española Way and Lincoln Road – See p57*

Left **Score** Right **Cactus**

🔟 Gay and Lesbian Venues

1 Twist
SoBe's largest gay venue has recently expanded, and there's something on every night of the week. Happy hour daily 1–9pm. ✪ *1057 Washington Ave, South Beach • 305-538-9478 • www.twistsobe.com • 1pm–5am daily*

2 Rise
Having experienced something of an identity crisis (formerly called Salvation, then 1771), this club continues to be an important part of the scene. ✪ *1771 West Ave, South Beach • 305-673-6508*

3 Laundry Bar
It's not all about suds at this much-frequented laundromat and full-service bar, alive with clean, cruisy locals and a throbbing dance beat. ✪ *721 Lincoln Lane at Meridian Ave • 305-531-7700*

4 Six Degrees
Food, drink, conversation. Café Miranda on Thursdays features music and martinis, and drag-show divas. Old South Beach nostalgia, so say those who were here in the 1990s. ✪ *685 Washington Ave, South Beach • 305-538-2212 • 7:30pm–1am, Tue–Sun*

5 Frankie & Johnny
Sunday Tea Dance is 3pm 'til 8pm, with 2-for-1 drinks; Friday is "All that Jazz"; Thursday is "Adrenaline" 2-for-1; then there's Go-Go in the Boom-Boom Room on Friday and Saturday. ✪ *1766 Bay Rd, South Beach • 305-695-0000*

6 Loading Zone
One of the heavier SoBe gay bars, weighing in mostly with the leather-Levis crowd, especially on Thursdays, Leather Nite. ✪ *1426A Alton Rd, South Beach • 305-531-5623*

7 Level
Calls itself "The Crown Jewel of South Beach Nightlife" and compares itself to Manhattan's Studio 54 in its heyday – it's not far off. Although not exclusively gay most of the time, Friday night certainly is. ✪ *1235 Washington Ave, South Beach • 305-604-0009 • www.levelnightclub.com*

8 Palace Bar and Grill
Formerly called Studio. Comfort food, artists' sanctuary, and bar, at the epicenter of gay life at the beach. ✪ *12th & Ocean, South Beach*

9 Cactus Tiki Bar
Happy Hours, special events every night – such as Latin Pool Party on Sundays, Noche Latina on Saturdays, and Industry Night on Tuesdays. Lots of gay professionals here after office hours. ✪ *2041 Biscayne Blvd • 305-438-0662 • www.thecactus.com*

10 Bash
This bar and lounge often hosts big events. Not exclusively gay at all, it is owned by Sean Penn and Mick Hucknall of Simply Red. ✪ *655 Washington Ave, South Beach • 305-538-0858*

For gay and lesbian venues in other parts of South Florida See pp52–3

Left **crobar** Center **Liquid** Right **Rumi**

🔟 Nightlife

1 Jazid
As the name would suggest, a more low-key choice, where you can listen to jazz and blues by candlelight, and, presumably, feed your id. ✆ *1342 Washington Ave, South Beach • 305-673-9372*

2 crobar
Housed in the former Cameo movie theater, this place employs high-tech prestidigitations to give you the sense of floating in a Surrealist's dreamworld. ✆ *1445 Washington Ave, South Beach • 305-531-8225 • www.crobarmiami.com*

3 Liquid
One of those SoBe clubs that people stand in line for, hoping to get selected on who-knows-what criteria. Inside, famous DJs keep the dance music at a fever pitch. ✆ *1532 Washington Ave, South Beach • 305-531-9411*

4 Rumi
Named as it is after the 13th-century Sufi mystic, you would expect to hear world music here, and you do, as well as house, trance, and other Buddha Bar-type lounge music. ✆ *330 Lincoln Rd, at Washington Ave, South Beach • 305-672-4353*

5 Opium Garden
Favored by the likes of Julia Roberts, this open-air venue is one of the most exclusive, so be prepared to wait. Mostly house music. ✆ *136 Collins Ave, at 1st St, South Beach • 305-531-5535*

6 Billboardlive
This newish high-tech performance space/recording studio is still searching for its own true identity but offers a mix of local and national acts, as well as DJs. ✆ *1500 Ocean Drive • 1-888-777-8886 or 305-538-2251 • www.billboardlive.com*

7 Lola
Sophisticated and a bit off the beaten path, Lola is a bar, lounge, and dance club all in one, designed for conversation, too. ✆ *247 23rd St, Miami Beach • 305-695-8697*

8 Rain
An upscale joint, with an in- and outside dance floor. Theme nights for a mixed crowd – ie not all gay. Loungy feel, with "bottle service," whereby you can order whole bottles of your favorite tipple to save time and effort. ✆ *323 23rd Street • 305-674-7447*

9 B.E.D.
Don't be a couch potato, go to B.E.D. instead. A bubbling mix of gay and straight, and, yes, there are actual beds for lounging on. ✆ *929 Washington Ave, South Beach • 305-532-9070*

10 Blue
Very laid back and cool, as in the color that dominates in this fun cocktail bar-and-club. Musical nights include tropical house, flashbacks, flow, and soul. ✆ *222 Española Way, South Beach • 305-534-1009*

For more on Miami's famous nightlife **See pp58–9**

Left **Van Dyke Café** Right **Terrace at the Tides**

Sidewalk Cafés

1 News Café
Numero uno on Ocean Drive, it's spacious and bustling, perfect for a drink, snack, or meal, and avid people-watching *(see also p8).* ✆ *800 Ocean Drive, at 8th St • $*

2 Mango's Tropical Café
Always hot, with upbeat music and a huge Floribbean menu. The action spills onto the sidewalk. ✆ *900 Ocean Drive, at 9th St • $$*

3 Clevelander
Facing the beach and on the sidewalk, there's always something going on here: listening to the live music, having something to eat, or just checking out the passersby. ✆ *1020 Ocean Beach • $*

4 Van Dyke
In the heart of Lincoln Road Mall, this is a prime spot for viewing the street parade. A good place for breakfast or lunch. Live jazz upstairs. ✆ *846 Lincoln Rd, South Beach • $*

5 Casa Salsa
Latin heartthrob Ricky Martin is the owner of this upscale Puerto Rican restaurant-bar. Live salsa music most of the time, as the name promises. ✆ *524 Ocean Drive, South Beach • $*

6 Pelican Café
Grab a seat on the outdoor patio and indulge yourself, just as Cameron Diaz, Antonio Banderas, and Johnny Depp have before you, in gawking at the SoBe procession and partaking of the Mediterranean-style delectables. ✆ *826 Ocean Drive, South Beach • $*

7 Front Porch Café
Many consider the breakfast here to be the best in South Beach. The atmosphere's homey, and the food's definitely worth the wait. ✆ *Penguin Hotel, 424 Ocean Drive, South Beach • $*

8 Larios on the Beach
Co-owned by pop Cuban songstress Gloria Estefan, it's *cocina cubana* prepared SoBe-style. Try the appetizer sampler for starters and some *rico mojitos* (yummy rum drink with mint leaves). ✆ *820 Ocean Drive, South Beach • $*

9 Terrace at the Tides
Very chic outdoor dining. Sit where celebrities have sat and tuck into the gourmet cooking: maybe lobster gazpacho or coconut mascarpone cheesecake. ✆ *1220 Ocean Drive, South Beach • $$*

10 Wet Willie's
This bar attracts a young, rowdy, post-beach crowd with its powerful frozen drinks with names such as Call Me a Cab. Nibbles to accompany the drinking include tasty fried calamari. ✆ *760 Ocean Drive, South Beach • $*

Around Miami – Miami Beach and Key Biscayne

Note: *Unless otherwise stated, all restaurants accept credit cards, have disabled access, and serve vegetarian meals*

Left **Mark's** Right **Tap Tap**

🔟 Restaurants

1 Mark's South Beach
Master-chef Mark Militello offers a wonderful fusion dining experience. Culinary stunners may include tenderloin of beef with roasted garlic purée on a polenta crouton. Desserts are extraordinary, too, and the wine selection perfect *(see also p60)*. ✆ Hotel Nash, 1120 Collins Ave, South Beach • 305-604-9050 • $$$

2 Tap Tap
Real Haitian food, some of it fiery with red chilies. Try the grilled conch with manioc or the shrimp in coconut sauce, with mango sorbet for dessert *(see also p60)*. ✆ 819 5th Street, South Beach • 305-672-2898 • $$

3 11th Street Diner
Classic diner from 1948, originally built in Pennsylvania. ✆ 1065 Washington Ave, at 11th St, South Beach • 305-534-6373 • $$

4 Joe's Stone Crab
Gloriously sweet stone crabs and a notorious wait to get in. Also fish – grilled, broiled, blackened, fried, or sautéed – pork, lamb, and steaks, and Miami's best Key lime pie *(see also p61)*. ✆ 11 Washington Ave, South Beach • 305-673-0365 • $$$

5 Escopazzo
Solid Italian fare. Swordfish carpaccio, asparagus flan, and risotto are hits *(see also p60)*. ✆ 1311 Washington Ave, South Beach • 305-674-9450 • $$$

6 Pacific Time
Recipes are delicious experimental meldings of Pacific Rim and Caribbean. Tuna tartar with Idaho potato chips, Szechuan grilled Florida Keys grouper, and broiled Florida grapefruit are typical *(see also p60)*. ✆ 915 Lincoln Rd, South Beach • 305-534-5979 • $$$

7 China Grill
A fusion cuisine pioneer. Portions are not pretentiously miniscule; tastes are light and cleverly composed. Try the sake-marinated chicken. ✆ 404 Washington Ave, S Beach • 305-534-2211 • $$$$

8 Abbey Dining Room
Set within an elegant Deco marvel *(see p147)* is a splendid place where food and art are happily confused. Don't miss bouillabaisse St. Tropez or the fantastic desserts. ✆ 300 21st St, South Beach • 305-531-0033 • $$$$

9 Bluemarine
Seafood is the forte here, done Southern Italian style. Try the pumpkin-shrimp soup or the zuppa di pesce for sensational pleasure. ✆ 754 Washington Ave, South Beach • 305-532-3678 • $$$$

10 Balans
An eclectic mix of Asian and Mediterranean influences, this chic, London-style café is popular, loud, and a SoBe standard-bearer. Great choice for a non-buffet Sunday brunch. ✆ 1022 Lincoln Road, South Beach • 305-534-9191 • $$

Price Categories

For a three-course meal for one with half a bottle of wine (or equivalent meal), taxes, and extra charges.	**$** under $20
	$$ $20–$40
	$$$ $40–$55
	$$$$ $55–$80
	$$$$$ over $80

Around Miami – Miami Beach and Key Biscayne

Following pages **Bright colors of an Art Deco-style beach patrol station on South Beach**

Left **Mosaic on dome of Gesu Church** Right **Bayside Marketplace**

Downtown and Little Havana

A LITTLE RUNDOWN, *this part of Miami is a foreign land for most Americans, but – if you are willing to make the cultural adjustment – it is a fascinating land. Here along the Miami River is where it all started in the late 1800s, but it took the arrival of Cuban exiles from the 1950s on for Miami to come into its own as a world player. On these brash streets, you will see that the influx from countries to the south has yet to abate and that the face of Miami is more Latino each day.*

🔟 Sights

1. Metro-Dade Cultural Center
2. Freedom Tower
3. US Federal Courthouse
4. Bayside Marketplace and Bayfront Park
5. NationsBank Tower
6. Gusman Center for the Performing Arts
7. Flagler Street
8. Gesu Church
9. Ingraham Building
10. Calle Ocho and Around

Tiles, Little Havana

Metro-Dade Cultural Center

1 Metro-Dade Cultural Center

Designed by the celebrated American architect Philip Johnson in 1982, the Mediterranean-style complex, set around a tiled plaza, incorporates the Miami Art Museum *(see p42)*; the Historical Museum of Southern Florida *(see pp42–3)*; and the Main Public Library, which contains four million books. ✎ *101 West Flagler St, Downtown • Map M2 • Library 9am-6pm Mon–Sat (to 9pm Thu), 1–5pm Sun*

2 Freedom Tower

Downtown's landmark was built in 1925 in the Mediterranean-Revival style, inspired by the Giralda, an 800-year-old bell tower in Seville, Spain. Initially home to the now-defunct *Miami Daily News*, its role and name changed in the 1960s, when it became the reception center to process more than 500,000 Cubans fleeing Castro. It was restored in 1988 to create a Cuban museum, but this failed to materialize, and the Tower is still empty. ✎ *600 Biscayne Blvd, Downtown • Map N1*

3 US Federal Courthouse

This imposing Neo-Classical edifice, finished in 1931, has hosted a number of high-profile trials, including that of Manuel Noriega, the former Panamanian president, in 1990. The spartan jail cell where he awaited trial on international drug-trafficking charges is also in this building. The main attraction is the second-floor mural entitled *Law Guides Florida's Progress*, designed by Denman Fink, famous for his work in Coral Gables. It depicts Florida's evolution from a tropical backwater to one of America's most prosperous states. ✎ *301 North Miami Ave, Downtown • Map N1 • 8am–5pm Mon–Fri, closed public hols & during major trials*

4 Bayside Marketplace and Bayfront Park

Curving around Miamarina, this shopping and entertainment complex is undeniably fun and the Downtown area's best attraction. It's not South Beach, but La Vida Loca echoes here, too, often with live salsa bands playing on the esplanade. Shops – including Guess?, Victoria's Secret, Structure, and Foot Locker – and 30 eateries, with

Freedom Tower

everything from ice cream to paella, make it a happening place. To the south, Bayfront Park, designed by Isamu Noguchi, is extensive and can provide a pleasant interlude of greenery, water, monuments, sculpture, and striking views. ✎ *401 Biscayne Blvd at 4th St, Downtown • Map P1–2 • www.bayside marketplace.com • 10am–10pm Mon–Thu, 10am–11pm Fri & Sat, 11am–9pm Sun*

Left **NationsBank Tower** Right **Ingraham Building**

5 NationsBank Tower

The city's most striking skyscraper is the work of architect I. M. Pei, perhaps most famous for putting the glass pyramid in the courtyard of the Louvre in Paris. This building is notable both during the day for its Op-Art horizontal banding across the stepped hemi-cylinders, and at night for the changing, sophisticated colors of its overall illumination. Built in 1983, the office building was known first as Centrust Tower, but it now bears the moniker of its current principal tenant. ◈ *International Place, 100 SE 1st St., Downtown • Map N2*

6 Gusman Center for the Performing Arts

Built in 1926, this theater has a fabulously ornate Moorish interior and is housed in the similarly colorful and festooned Olympia Building. It began as a vaudeville theater, where Rudy Vallee used to perform, and Elvis Presley also gigged here. Inside, the hall looks like an Arabian Nights palace, with turrets, towers, intricate columns, and a crescent moon and stars in the ceiling. Buy a ticket to anything just to see it. ◈ *174 E Flagler St, at SE 1st Ave., Downtown • Map N2 • Box Office 305-372-0925*

Gusman Center

Gateway to Latin America

Two-thirds of Miami's population is of Hispanic origin. Pick up the *Miami Herald* and you'll see that the news of the day in Caracas, Bogotá, Managua, and above all Havana is given top billing. All these connections, for good or ill, have made Miami the US kingpin in dealing with Latin and South America.

7 Flagler Street

Flagler is Downtown Miami's main drag – loud, bright, busy, and lined with small shops and street peddlers. Pop into the Galería International Mall (243 East Flagler Street, at SE 2nd Avenue) for cheap and tasty ethnic snacks, while on the next block is the stylish Gusman Center. On East Flagler Street at NE 2nd Avenue, look for the Alfred I. DuPont Building (1937–9), a paean to Art Deco in the Depression Moderne style. ◈ *Map N2*

8 Gesu Church

This Mediterranean-Revival building in the Spanish Colonial style (built 1922) is the oldest Catholic church in Miami. Dozens of masses are held every week, in English and Spanish. The church is noted for its stained-glass

Gesu Church

windows, which were made in Munich, Germany. The ceiling mural was restored in its entirety by a lone Nicaraguan refugee in the late 1980s. ✆ *118 NE 2nd St, Downtown • Map N1 • 305-379-1424*

⑨ Ingraham Building

Completed in 1926, this is a kind of Neo-Renaissance work: the building's twelve stories are clad in Indiana limestone and its roof sheathed in Spanish tiles. The interior is opulent, featuring a lavish ceiling decorated in gold leaf, with the building's insignia cast in brass. The lobby's light fixtures, the mailbox, and the office directory are all original. Picked out in gold on the elevator are scenes of South Florida wildlife. ✆ *25 SE 2nd Ave, at E. Flagler St, Downtown • Map N2*

⑩ Calle Ocho and Around

A slice of Cuban culture, liberally spiced up with all sorts of other Hispanic and Caribbean influences. Since Castro's Communist revolution in Cuba, Miami has become ever more Cubanized by wave after wave of immigrants from the embattled island they still long for as home (see pp14–15).

A Trip Through Calle Ocho

Mid-morning

First stop, if you like a cigar, is **El Crédito** *(see pp14 & 88)* on SW 11th Ave. Just a few doors along you'll find the **Botánica El Aguila Vidente** *(see p88)*. Let your eye wander over the shop's plethora of paraphernalia, most of all the colorful plaster statues.

Next stop is at SW 13th Avenue, to pay your respects to fallen Cuban freedom fighters at the **Brigade 2506 Memorial Eternal Flame** *(see p14)*, before a sortie into the delightful fruit market at 1334, **Los Pinareños Fruteria** *(see p88)*.

At the corner of SW 15th Ave, peek in on **Domino Park** *(see p15)* where there's always at least one game going on. And now comes time to stop for coffee and maybe a snack at the wonderful **Exquisito** *(see p89)*. Try to grab one of the vibrantly colored tables outside.

Late morning

Continuing on to the next block, at 1652, take in the exciting Latin American art at the **Agustín Gaínza Gallery** *(see p88)*, where you're likely to meet the affable artist himself.

After that, try a free-form ramble of discovery – but don't miss the gaudy entrance to **La Casa de los Trucos** *(see p88)*, at 1343 – and when it's time for lunch, head for **El Pescador** *(see p89)*, also on the north side of Calle Ocho. This is the place to go for delicious fish.

Left **Latino theater, Calle Ocho** Right **Metromover**

🔟 Walks, Drives, and Viewpoints

1 Bayside Marketplace
Adjacent to the impressive American Airlines Arena, this complex feels part Disney theme-park, part international bazaar. Right on the waterfront, it's always good for a stroll *(see p83)*.

2 Flagler Street
Walking through the heart of Downtown Miami is reminiscent of a marketplace you might encounter in Latin America – colorful, brash, rather seedy – and none too safe at night *(see p84)*.

3 Calle Ocho Walk
The area between 11th and 17th Avenues is excellent for walking. You can check out ethnic shops and sample various Cuban delicacies along the way *(see p85)*.

4 Architectural Walk
The buildings highlighted on pages 83–5 are lined up over about six blocks along NE–SE 1st and 2nd avenues. Another building worth a look is the Neo-Classical-Revival Miami-Dade County Courthouse, three blocks away. Don't miss the ceiling mosaics in the impressive lobby. ◈ *Map N1–2*

5 A Drive through Little Havana
To get the overall feel and extent of Little Havana, it's best to drive, from José Martí Park in the west to about 34th Avenue in the east, where the Woodlawn Cemetery and Versailles Restaurant are located *(see p15)*.

6 Views of Downtown
Some of the best views of Downtown are afforded from the freeways. Coming across MacArthur Causeway from South Beach, you'll get some dazzling perspectives, especially at night. The finest view of the skyline is from the Rickenbacker Causeway. ◈ *Maps P1 & M6*

7 A Ride on the Metromover
The Metromover consists of two elevated loops around Downtown, so it's a great way to get an overview of the area *(see p137)*.

8 A Calle Ocho Café
The Exquisito Cafetería *(see p89)* is the best on the street and a wonderful place to listen to the music and watch the fascinating street life all around.

9 A Stroll in José Martí Park
This charming little park by the Miami River is graced with colonnades and pavilions, Spanish-style clusters of street lamps, palm trees, and an excellent children's playground. ◈ *Map M2*

10 A Stroll in Bayfront Park
Right on beautiful Biscayne Bay, Noguchi designed this park "as a wedge of art in the heart of the New World." Here, in addition to Noguchi's sculptures you will find lush greenery, a small sand beach, tropical rock garden, cascading fountain, palms, and olive trees. ◈ *Map P1–2*

Left **Histórico Teatro Martí** Right **Gusman Center**

Lively Latino Arts Venues

1 Teatro de Bellas Artes
This Calle Ocho venue presents eight Spanish plays and musicals a year. Most of the plays are Spanish originals, but there are also plays in translation, such as Tennessee Williams' *A Streetcar Named Desire*. 🖎 *2173 SW 8th St • 305-325-0515*

2 Porcão
This Brazilian supper club and bar features some of the best live Brazilian music in town, especially when sultry singer Rose Max performs: Thur and Fri Happy Hours. 🖎 *Four Ambassadors Hotel, 801 Brickell Bay Dr • 305-373-2777*

3 Cultura del Lobo
The Performance Series presents music, dance, film, and visual arts, with an emphasis on contemporary works and solo theater performers. 🖎 *Miami-Dade Community College, Wolfson Campus 300 NE 2nd Ave, at NE 3rd St*

4 Teatro Ocho
Home to the Hispanic Theater Guild, which regularly presents Spanish-language theater. Its directors try to choose topical plays that will stir public opinion and become a force for renewal in the Cuban community. 🖎 *2101 SW 8th St*

5 Histórico Teatro Martí
Cuban exile comedy and Spanish productions of musicals such as *The Wizard of Oz*. 🖎 *420 SW 8th St • 305-545-7866*

6 Performance Space 742
The first Saturday of every month is "Surreal Saturday" in the experimental performance arena, with four featured performances of music, dance, theater, and poetry inside, and a DJ artist scratching tunes outside. Also rhumba and drumming jam sessions. 🖎 *742 SW 16th Ave • 305-324-0585*

7 Manuel Artime Theater
A former Baptist church, this Downtown facility has been converted into an 800-seat state-of-the-art theater and is the home of the Miami Hispanic Ballet, which produces the annual International Ballet Festival. 🖎 *900 SW First St • 305-575-5057*

8 Gusman Center for the Performing Arts
The major Downtown venue *(see p84)* often features Latin American performances of all types, including films during the annual Miami Film Festival.

9 Café Gallery 2000
Live Latin music is performed most nights in this wonderful, stimulating space *(see p89)*.

10 Casa Panza
Great flamenco performances several nights a week at this authentic Spanish restaurant right in the Cuban heart of Calle Ocho *(see p89)*.

*Miami's more mainstream arts venues are on **pp38–9***

Left **Botánica El Aguila Vidente** Center **Agustin Gaínza Gallery** Right **Los Pinareños Fruteria**

Cuban/Latino Shopping

1 Botánica El Aguila Vidente
The most atmospheric and mysterious of the botánicas along the main section of Calle Ocho *(see pp15 & 48)*.

2 Agustín Gaínza Gallery
The gallery's namesake, a celebrated Cuban artist, shows his works here, as well as those of other contemporary Cuban and Latin American artists. ✆ 1652 SW 8th St • 305-644-5855

3 Old Cuba, The Collection
This welcoming little store specializes in Cuban art, music, books, and clothing, as well as dominoes, coffee-makers, and fine cigars. The owner, Jackie Perez, also promotes a mini-street-festival of the arts held on the last Friday of each month. ✆ 561 SW 8th St • 305-643-6269

4 El Crédito
A raggedy old factory, where you can watch cigars being rolled and breathe in the sweet perfume of pure tobacco *(see p14)*.

5 Los Pinareños Fruteria
A delightful fruit market for finding all sorts of exotic Caribbean produce, such as mamey and small "apple" bananas. There's also a wonderful café and fresh juice bar. ✆ 1334 SW 8th St

6 La Casa de los Trucos
If you're in town for Carnaval or Halloween, this is the place to come for all your costuming needs. From the most predictable to the most bizarre, this shop has a vast inventory and excellent prices, to buy or rent. ✆ 1343 SW 8th St • 305-858-5029

7 Nicaragua Bakery
Both a bakery and a snack bar-café for trying typical Nicaraguan treats such as fried plantain, fried pork rinds, *nacatamal* (Nicaraguan tamale), or *pan de pico* (a very rich cheese bread). ✆ 1167–9 SW 8th St

8 Café Gallery 2000
This all-purpose cultural entertainment and refreshment center features upbeat, Picasso-esque paintings on the walls, custom framing, a restoration service, live music, and a bistro. ✆ 1644 SW 8th St • 305-642-4292

9 Mediterranean Gallery
A pleasing array of imported ceramics. The pottery and garden decorations come from Spain, Colombia, and Mexico, while the columns and mouldings are made by the proprietors themselves. ✆ 3178 SW 8th St • 305-644-9595

10 Casino Records
There are at least seven record shops between 11th and 17th streets, each with outside speakers, keeping the street energy on high. Cubans seem to live for music, and Casino does its level best to provide the Latin sounds in the largest quantities. ✆ 1208 SW 8th St • 305-856-6888

Left **Versailles** Right **El Atlacatl**

🔟 Cuban/Latino Food

1 Versailles
A Little Havana institution, Versailles is actually a Cuban diner in a very sleek guise *(see pp15 & 60)*. ◈ *3555 SW 8th St, at SW 35th Ave • 305-444-0240 • $$*

2 Garcia's Seafood Grille & Fish Market
A family-run eatery with a friendly atmosphere, in- and outdoors, though you might have a bit of a wait. Great grouper chowder, and conch salad. ◈ *398 NW North River Dr • 305-375-0765 • $$*

3 Exquisito Restaurant
The most authentic and affordable on the street, where locals go every day. All the gritty Cuban fare, like brain fritters and horse beef stew, but also things "gringos" can relish, such as Cajun lobster or shrimp, or pork chops. ◈ *1510 SW 8th Street (Calle Ocho), Little Havana • 305 643-0227 • $*

4 El Atlacatl
The cuisine of El Salvador, served in a spacious, cheerful setting. Pleasant murals, and a menu that leans toward chicken and seafood. ◈ *3199 SW 8th St • 305-649-8000 • $$*

5 El Pescador
All fish, all the time, with daily specials, such as seafood soup, fried snapper, and yellow rice with seafood on Fridays. Salads and other sides, such as black beans and plantain. ◈ *1543 SW 8th St • 305-541-9224 • $*

6 Casa Panza
A picturesque Spanish restaurant, well known for its fine paella and authentic flamenco show. Rooms are cozy, with different flamenco performers several nights of the week. ◈ *1620 SW 8th St • 305-643-5343 • $$$*

7 Old Lisbon
A taste of Portuguese cuisine, with *sardinhas assadas* (grilled sardines), *salada polvo* (octopus salad), mussels, squid, and assorted cheeses. ◈ *1698 SW 22nd St • 305-854-0039 • $$$*

8 El Crucero
Old-fashioned hospitality, Cuban style, and amazing cooking. Daily specials are listed on the board. Don't miss the creamy *natilla*, a sweet custard with a caramelized top, which rounds off a meal perfectly. ◈ *7050 SW 8th St • 305-262-1966 • $*

9 Cancun Grill
Mexican food at its best. Try the fish ceviche, the *taquitos rancheros*, and the Cuban-Mex plantain nachos. ◈ *15406 NW 77th Court, Miami Lakes • 305-826-8571 • $*

10 Guayacan
Cozy and unpretentious, this is Cuban fare with a zingy Nicaraguan twist. Try the *pescado a la Tipitapa*, a whole red snapper deep-fried and drenched in a sauce of onions and peppers. Wonderful soups as well. ◈ *1933 SW 8th St • 305-649-2015 • $$*

> **Note:** Unless otherwise stated, all restaurants accept credit cards, have disabled access, and serve vegetarian meals

Left **Vintage goods shop** Center **Design District** Right **1930s police car, American Police Museum**

North of Downtown

THE AREAS NORTH *of Miami Beach and Downtown are an irreconcilable juxtaposition of urban sprawl and urban chic, of downtrodden ethnic and high-flying elite. Little is actually scenic, although the beaches are among the area's greatest. Indeed, much of northern Miami has the reputation of a slum. There's local color to be discovered, but the vibes can be less than welcoming, and you should be careful. Still, some of Greater Miami's most scintillating sights, including one of the oldest buildings in the Americas, and fine dining can also be found here.*

Showpiece, Mynaya shop

Sights

1 Ancient Spanish Monastery
2 Little Haiti
3 Opa-Locka
4 American Police Hall of Fame & Museum
5 Bal Harbour
6 Museum of Contemporary Art
7 Design District
8 Hialeah Park
9 Arch Creek Park and Museum
10 Greynolds Park

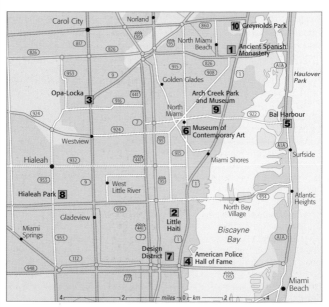

Take extra care when visiting Opa-Locka and Little Haiti, and when driving through Hialeah. Avoid Liberty City and Overtown.

Left **Iron ornamentation, Ancient Spanish Monastery** Right **Façade in Little Haiti**

Ancient Spanish Monastery

This is the oldest European-tradition building in the Western Hemisphere, originally built in 1133–41 near Segovia, Spain. In 1925, William Randolph Hearst bought the magnificent cloisters, had the structures dismantled stone by stone, packed in some 11,000 wooden crates, then shipped to the US. After many trials and tribulations, the stones were finally reassembled here in the early 1950s at a cost of $1.5 million. See page 93 for a suggested tour. ⊗ *16711 W Dixie Hwy, North Miami Beach • Map H1 • 305-945-1461 • www. spanishmonastery.com • 9am–5pm Mon–Sat, 1:30–5pm Sun • Adm*

Little Haiti

Little Haiti is not so much dangerous as disconcerting – to see so much poverty just steps away from such wealth. The one attempt at promoting tourism was the Caribbean Marketplace. Though critically acclaimed, it has had mixed success. ⊗ *NE 2nd Ave, from about NE 55th to NE 80th • Map G2 • Marketplace at 5927 NE 2nd Ave*

Opa-Locka

Nicknamed the "Baghdad of Dade County," the fantasy follies of this now-depressed district were the brainchild of Glenn Curtiss in the 1920s. All in pink, with minarets, burnished domes, and keyhole arches, the restored City Hall is the best example left. (But don't stray far from it.) ⊗ *Cnr NW 27th Ave & NW 135th St • Map G2*

American Police Hall of Fame & Museum

A display about Gangland's most notorious criminals, a Robocop, police weapons, and a gas chamber are among the exhibits. The huge memorial engraved with the names of 5,000 American police officers who have died in the line of duty is very moving. ⊗ *3801 Biscayne Blvd • Map G2 • 305-573-0070 10am–5:30pm daily • Adm*

City Hall, Opa-Locka

For personal security tips **See p139**

Haulover Beach Park, north of Bal Harbour

5 Bal Harbour

The Barrier islands north of Miami Beach are occupied mainly by posh residential areas, and this is the poshest. Known for its flashy hotels and one of the swankiest malls anywhere, Bal Harbour is said to have more millionaires per capita than any other city in the US. Bal Harbour Shops – note the British spelling – is a determinedly snooty place in a tropical setting, whose tone is set by the wealthy grandes dames and the security staff in neo-colonial uniforms and pith helmets. Elsewhere along 96th Street, you'll find galleries, gourmet shops, and a swarm of plastic surgery studios. ✆ *Map H2*

6 Museum of Contemporary Art

The museum (MOCA) opened its state-of-the-art building to the public in 1996. It's known for its provocative exhibitions and for

Museum of Contemporary Art

Class and Culture Clash

Greater Miami is a bubbling cauldron of cultural diversity. Many endemically underprivileged African-American communities lie within a stone's throw of exclusive shops. In other areas, impoverished recent immigrants – from Cuba, Haiti, and other Central American countries – eke out miserable existences in huddled quarters of endless urban blight.

seeking a fresh approach in examining the art of our time. ✆ *770 NE 125th St • Map G2 • 305-893-6211 • www. mocanomi.org • 11am–5pm Tue–Sat, noon–5pm Sun • Adm • Tours on Sat at 2pm*

7 Design District

It started out as a pineapple grove, but from the 1920s this zone was being called Decorators' Row because of the design stores that had moved in. For a while in the '80s, due to high crime, the area fell on hard times, but things are picking up again, and top-end design, furniture, and fixture shops once again rule. Photographers and artists have been moving here, too, to escape the high rents of South Beach. ✆ *Nr Buena Vista between NE 36th–41st Sts and from NE 2nd to N Miami Aves • Map G2*

Design District

8 Hialeah Park

This raceway has been running thoroughbred horses for over 75 years. Whether it's got a race on or not, the Park is open year-round for sightseeing – the French Mediterranean-Revival-style structure, and the landscaped grounds with a flock of 400 pink flamingos make it one of the great oases of Greater Miami. Unfortunately, the rest of Hialeah has not fared so well: endless concrete, junk-food joints, and terrible traffic. ✥ Map G2 • 305-885-8000 • www.hialeahpark.com

9 Arch Creek Park and Museum

Created around a natural limestone bridge formation, this location used to be part of an important Native American trail. A museum/nature center contains artifacts left by those peoples. Naturalists will be your guides as they point out native birds, animals, insects, and trees. ✥ 1855 NE 135 St • Map G2

10 Greynolds Park

An oak-shaded haven for runners, golfers, and other outdoor enthusiasts, Greynolds Park is landscaped with native and exotic plants, including mangrove, royal palm, palmetto, pampas grass, sea grape, and gumbo limbo. You'll also find beach volleyball courts, a children's playground, and plenty of picnic tables. ✥ 17530 W Dixie Hwy • Map H1 • Adm weekends

A Tour of the Ancient Spanish Monastery

Morning

Drive north from central Miami on Highway 1 (also called Biscayne Blvd). The road is lined with shops – stop off at any that catch your eye. Turn left on NE 163rd St, then right onto W Dixie Hwy (also NE 22nd Ave). The **Ancient Spanish Monastery** (see also p91) is on the right after the canal.

You may well feel a sense of awe as you walk around this beautiful little piece of medieval Europe on US soil. Even European visitors, who have visited many such buildings in their homeland, might still marvel at the dedication of Hearst to put it here.

For the best route through the grounds, start at the gift shop/museum, exit to the patio, through the gardens, cloisters, interior rooms, culminating with the chapel, and back through the gift shop.

Among the notable sights are an 800-year-old birdbath, a life-size statue of the Spanish king Alphonso VII (the monastery was constructed to commemorate one of his victories over the Moors), and two of only three known surviving round stained-glass windows from the 12th century.

Afternoon

In keeping with the Spanish-inspired theme, eat at nearby **Paquito's Mexican Restaurant** (see p95) and take a detour along NE 2nd Ave through colorful **Little Haiti** (see p91) on your way back.

Left **Vierge Miracle lotions and potions store** Right **Collectibles at Divine Trash**

🔟 Unusual Shops

1 Vierge Miracle & Botànica Saint Philippe
Right in the heart of Little Haiti, it doesn't get more authentic than this. It's helpful if you can speak French to find out more about the myriad soaps, sprays, and lotions. ⊗ *5910 NE 2nd Ave*

2 Minar
Oriental rugs – some very old and exquisite – art, textiles, wall-hangings, and beautiful ceramics from Central Asia and China. The atmosphere is delightfully Eastern, right down to the tea served. ⊗ *6667 Biscayne Blvd*

3 Divine Trash
All sorts of antiques, art, collectibles, and various found objects. The upbeat, charming proprietor, Donna Ashby, is something of a local celebrity. Don't miss her orchid garden and the great day spa upstairs *(see no.4)*. ⊗ *7244 Biscayne Blvd*

4 Jacqué, Inc.
Environmentally conscious, aromatherapy day spa, with various treatments and a line of natural fiber clothing, herbal lotions, and organic foods. ⊗ *7242 Biscayne Blvd • 1-800-444-1046*

5 Art By God
Impressive mineral/nature store, with dinosaur fossils, natural and carved semiprecious gemstones, insects, shells, butterflies, skulls, animal mounts, etc. ⊗ *3705 Biscayne Blvd*

6 Urban Garden
A wonderful space, chock full of architectural antiques, garden relics, studio props, and indefinable treasures. ⊗ *235 NE 79th St*

7 It's A Take
Everything needed for a lifetime of romantic dinners: place settings, linens, decorative objects galore, gourmet treats, and a florist. ⊗ *6924 Biscayne Blvd*

8 Mynaya
Off the back garden of Sokya restaurant *(No.1, right)* is this lovely little shop featuring imported clothing and accessories. ⊗ *55th St Stn, 5580 NE 4th Ct*

9 Diable En Deuil Botánica
If you want luck or for your lover to behave, there are ways… and this is the place to find them: Haitian powders, potions, and iconographic figures abound, some of them very sexually graphic. ⊗ *8009 NE 2nd Ave*

10 Naomi Variety Store
For a taste of the Islands, stop by this earthy little shack selling tropical fruits, vegetables, flour, etc. ⊗ *5526 NE 2nd Ave*

Mynaya

Price Categories

For a three-course meal for one with half a bottle of wine (or equivalent meal), taxes, and extra charges.

$	under $20
$$	$20–$40
$$$	$40–$55
$$$$	$55–$80
$$$$$	over $80

La Paloma

🔟 Places to Eat

1 Soyka
Run by the same fellow as the News Café (see p8), this is a huge, bistro-like setting with an adventurous Italianesque fusion menu. The sesame-seared salmon with spinach, shiitakes, and sweet soy sauce is not only alliterative but also simply sensationally scrumptious. ✆ 5556 NE 4th Ct • 305-759-3117• $$

Cafe del Mar

2 Da Ermanno Ristorante
A big favorite with discerning locals. Appetizers, pastas, pizzas, and main courses, such as clams and linguine, and eggplant Parmesan. ✆ 6927 Biscayne Blvd • 305-759-2001 • $$

3 Andiamo!
A jaunty little place that specializes in brick-oven pizza, choice panini, salads, and desserts. Homemade cannoli and other goodies for dessert. ✆ 5600 Biscayne Blvd • 305-762-5751 • $

4 Café del Mar
Spanish name, rustic nautical New England décor, French-style seafood. Try the egg crêpe-wrapped Biscayne rolls. ✆ 8699 Biscayne Blvd • 305-759-1100 • $$

5 Hanna Gourmet Diner
Homemade soups; inventive salads, such as tomato with fennel and goat cheese; snapper française; steak au poivre; and an unforgettable fruit tart. ✆ 13951 Biscayne Blvd • 305-947-2255 • $$

6 Chef Allen's
International fusion artistry at its finest. The Indian-influenced dishes include "cowboy" steak with tamarind and chili and lobster-crab cakes with fruit chutney. Hazelnut "Kit-Kat" bars make an unusual finish. ✆ 19088 NE 29th Ave • 305-935-2900 • $$$$$

7 La Paloma
Old-World ornate, borderline kitsch décor. A superb house salad comes with every entrée. Try oysters Rockefeller, trout amandine, or veal Milanese. ✆ 10999 Biscayne Blvd • 305-891-0505 • $$$

8 Paquito's Mexican Restaurant
Expect sumptuously fresh tortilla soup, steak Paquitos sautéed in a creamy jalapeño and onion sauce, and a yummy mole verde. ✆ 16265 Biscayne Blvd • 305-947-5027 • $$

9 Tulipano Centodieci
More Old World allure and solid fare such as octopus with polenta, or chicken Scarpariello. ✆ 11052 Biscayne Blvd • 305-893-4211 • $$$

10 Picanha's Grille
Always packed with Brazilians and others. Dishes include meaty linguincinha sausages and rich sautéed prawns. ✆ 2286 NE 123rd St • 305-895-9009 • $$

Note: Unless otherwise stated, all restaurants have disabled access, accept credit cards, and serve vegetarian meals

Left **Venetian Pool** Center **One of Merrick's fantasies** Right **Lowe Art Museum**

Coral Gables and Coconut Grove

CORAL GABLES AND COCONUT GROVE, *taken together, constitute one of the most upscale neighborhoods in Greater Miami. The former is actually a separate city, while the latter is a district of Miami, its oldest, and the site of the Miami City Hall. Coral Gables was one of the nation's first "planned" cities and is consistently posh from end to end. Coconut Grove is a more variegated mosaic, historically the focus of Miami's intellectual, bohemian community but also incorporating the blighted "Black Grove", where the descendants of Bahamian workers often live in real squalor.*

🔟 Sights

1. Biltmore Hotel
2. Venetian Pool
3. International Villages
4. Miracle Mile
5. Lowe Art Museum
6. CocoWalk
7. Villa Vizcaya
8. Barnacle State Historic Site
9. Peacock Park
10. Dinner Key

Exhibit, Midori Gallery

Previous pages **Villa Vizcaya**

Biltmore Hotel

1 Biltmore Hotel

George Merrick was one of the visionaries who made Florida into what it is; this lavish hotel stands as a monument to his taste and grand ideas. Herculean pillars line the grand lobby, and from the terrace you can survey the largest hotel swimming pool in the country. Johnny Weismuller, the first movie Tarzan, used to teach swimming here, and the likes of Al Capone, Judy Garland, and the Duke and Duchess of Windsor came in its heyday. Weekly tours of the hotel and grounds depart from the front desk *(see also pp18 & 146).* ✎ *Map F3*

2 Venetian Pool

One of the loveliest and most evocative of Merrick's additions to his exotic vision for Coral Gables. The pool is fed by springs and was the site of at least one movie starring Esther Williams, the 1940s water-ballet beauty *(see also p18–19 & 64).* ✎ *Map G3*

3 International Villages

Merrick's architectural flights of fancy still add a special grace note to beautiful, upscale Coral Gables. All are private homes, but you can drive by and take in their unique charms *(see also pp18–19).* ✎ *Map G4*

4 Miracle Mile

In 1940, a developer hyped the town's main shopping street by naming it Miracle Mile (a mile if you walk up one side and down the other). Colorful canopies adorn shops as prim and proper as their clientele. Buildings of note are Merrick's Colonnade Building, at 169, with its splendid rotunda; the Doc Dammers' Saloon, with great photos of old Coral Gables; and, on nearby Salzedo Street at Aragon Avenue, the Old Police and Fire Station, 1939, with square-jawed sculpted firemen. ✎ *Coral Way between Douglas and Le Jeune • Map F–G3*

5 Lowe Art Museum

Greater Miami's finest art museum boasts solid collections of ancient and modern world art *(see pp20–21).* ✎ *Map F3*

Left **Façade, International Villages** Right **Colonnade Building, Miracle Mile**

For more about George Merrick's fabulous buildings in Coral Gables **See pp18–19**

Left **CocoWalk mall** Right **Villa Vizcaya**

6 CocoWalk

This compact, two-story center is the heart of Coconut Grove Village, and features some good shopping, dining, and entertainment. The atmosphere is, in fact, that of a village. People are hanging out, zipping by on in-line skates and bikes, checking each other out. Often live music is happening right in the middle of it all. The main attraction in the evening is probably the multiplex cinema. ◈ 3015 Grand Avenue • Map G3 • 305-443-7722 • www.cocowalk.com

7 Villa Vizcaya

One of the most historic and beautiful places in the Greater Miami area; this icon of the city's cultural life is not to be missed (see pp16–17). ◈ Map G3

8 Barnacle State Historic Site

Hidden from the highway by a tropical hardwood hammock (mound), this is Dade County's

Barnacle State Historic Site

Grand Plans in the Grove and Gables

The area called Coconut Grove was the first in the Miami area to be settled. Following the Civil War, in 1868, Edmund Beasley responded to the Homestead Act of 1862, claiming his 160 acres of land here, his free if he could only manage to live on it for five years and make some improvements, which he did. It took the genius of George Merrick, some 60 years later, to dream the notion of preplanning an entire ideal city – Coral Gables (see pp18–19).

oldest home. It was designed and built in 1891 by Commodore Ralph Munroe, who made his living as a boat builder and a wrecker (salvager). In fact, wood from shipwrecks was used to build the house, and it was inventively laid out to allow the circulation of air, all-important in those days before air-conditioning. Rooms are stuffed with old family heirlooms, old tools, and wonderful early appliances. ◈ 3485 Main Highway, Coconut Grove • Map G3 • 305-448-9445 • www.gate.net/~barnacle • 9am–4pm Fri, Sat, Sun, Mon; by reservation Tue, Wed, Thu • Closed national holidays • 1-hour tours at 10 & 11:30am, 1 & 2:30pm • Adm

9 Peacock Park

In the 1960s, this was where the Grove hippies grooved, and on weekends now and when there's a festival, some of the old magic gets temporarily resurrected. The park is named after Charles and Isabella Peacock, who built the area's first hotel, the Peacock Inn, which at the time was the only hotel between Palm Beach and Key West. The park is now largely a baseball field, and there's also a rustic Chamber of Commerce building. ® *2820 MacFarlane Ave, at Bayshore Drive, Coconut Grove • Map G3*

10 Dinner Key

The name derives from the early days when settlers had picnics here. In the 1930s, Pan American Airways transformed Dinner Key into the busiest seaplane base in the US. It was also the departure point for Amelia Earhart's doomed round-the-world flight in 1937. The airline's sleek Streamline Moderne terminal houses the Miami City Hall, and the hangars are now mostly boatyards, though one is the famous Monty's Stone Crab Seafood House and Raw Bar *(see p105)*. The marina here is now the most prestigious in Miami, so walk along and enjoy inspecting the yachts berthed here. ® *5 Bayshore Drive, Coconut Grove • Map G3*

Dinner Key

A Tour of Coconut Grove Village

Morning

🕐 This walk is designed for Friday–Monday, because it begins with a tour of the **Barnacle State Historic Site**. Try to get there for the 10am tour, and notice the distinctive roof, which gives the house its name.

As you exit, turn left and go down to the corner of Devon Road to enjoy the Mission-style **Plymouth Congregational Church** *(see p47)*, built in 1916. If they're open, pop into the back gardens.

Now walk back along Main Highway several blocks to 3500, the **Coconut Grove Playhouse** *(see p38)*, a handsome Mediterranean-Revival building that dominates the corner at Charles Avenue. Continue along Main Highway to the next street, then stop for lunch and some top-notch people-watching at the every-busy **Green Street Café** *(p102)*.

Afternoon

After lunch, walk up Commodore Plaza to visit 3168, the **Midori Gallery** *(p104)*. Afterwards, continue on to Grand Avenue and turn right; go down a couple of blocks to the major intersection and cross the street into the shopping mecca **CocoWalk**.

On the next block, Rice Street, look up to admire the fanciful façade of **The Streets of Mayfair** mall *(p104)*. To finish off your tour, visit **Borders** *(p104)* on the corner of Grand Avenue and Mary Street for a drink and maybe a book on Grove history.

Left **CocoWalk entrance** Right **Johnny Rockets**

Special Places and Events

1 Books and Books
One of Greater Miami's best bookstores, set amid graceful arcades *(see p104)*.

2 CocoWalk
A compact shopping and entertainment center right in the heart of Coco Village – always something or someone to catch the eye *(see p100)*.

3 Johnny Rockets
This 1950s-style diner opposite CocoWalk is always jumping. Order a burger and fries and watch the whole of the Grove go by sooner or later. ⚘ *3036 Grand, cnr of Main Hwy, Coconut Grove*

4 Green Street Café
Almost always crowded, this corner venue is another prime people-watching spot in the Grove. Sit and sip a drink or order up a full meal. ⚘ *3110 Commodore Plaza, Coconut Grove • 305-444-0244*

5 King Mango Strut
An outrageous local tradition that sends up the year's events and celebrities, harking back to the days when the Grove was a haven for intellectuals and eccentrics. The party climaxes with a concert and dance in Peacock Park. ⚘ *Last week of December • Starts at Main Hwy & Commodore Plaza, Coconut Grove • 305-445-1865*

6 Coconut Grove Arts Festival
Perhaps Greater Miami's best such festival, attracting throngs of visitors who come to eat, drink, listen to concerts in Peacock Park, and browse among 300 arts and crafts booths. ⚘ *Three days over the third weekend in Feb • Throughout the Grove, especially Bayshore and Peacock Parks • www.coconutgroveartsfest.com*

7 Miami-Bahamas Goombay Festival
A Bahamian party that includes a parade, Island food, Caribbean music, and *junkanoo* dancers parading through the streets. It claims to be the biggest African-American heritage festival in the US. ⚘ *First weekend in Jun • Throughout the Grove • 305-3567-1399*

8 Miami International Orchid Show
Florida has become one of the world centers for the orchid industry. More than half a million blooms are displayed at this show. ⚘ *Early Mar • Coconut Grove Convention Center, 2700 S. Bayshore Drive, at SW 27th Ave • 305-255-3656*

9 Italian Renaissance Festival
Staged in the perfect backdrop of the Vizcaya gardens *(see pp16–17)*: jousting, juggling, jesters, lutes, dulcimers, etc. ⚘ *4 days in Mar • 305-250-9133*

10 Columbus Day Regatta
Some 600 sailboats run this race. ⚘ *Mid-Oct • Coral Reef Yacht Club to Elliot Key • www.columbusdayregatta.net*

For more on Miami's colorful festivals See pp40–41

Left **Chinese Village, designed by Merrick** Right **Coral Gables Merrick House**

🔟 Walks, Drives, and Historic Sites

1 Miracle Mile
Though not really quite a mile, nor particularly miraculous, this street and parallel ones are mostly about nice shops and elegant eateries *(see p99)*.

2 Coconut Grove Village
This is a place to walk *(see p101)*, but it's probably best not to venture more than a few blocks west of CocoWalk ("Black Grove," sadly, is uninviting). 🗺 *Map G3*

3 Merrick Villages
Driving around Coral Gables to take in these charming residences, done up in the styles of various national and regional cultures, will take perhaps a couple of hours *(see pp18–19)*.

4 Barnacle State Historic Site
This unusual house, lived in by the descendants of its original builder until 1973, is the area's oldest, built in 1891 *(see p100)*.

5 Villa Vizcaya
A recreation of a 16th-century Italian villa with formal gardens *(see pp16–17)*.

Vizcaya grotto

6 Biltmore Hotel
Inimitably beautiful and grand, this is one of the world's most gorgeous hotels, opened in 1926 *(see p99)*.

7 Congregational Church
Merrick's deliciously Baroque paean to his father, a Congregational minister, was Coral Gables' first church and remains the city's most beautiful *(see p19)*.

8 Venetian Pool
Considered the world's most beautiful public swimming pool. You could spend half a day enjoying its charms *(see pp18 & 99)*.

9 Coral Gables Merrick House
The boyhood home of George Merrick *(see p19)* has been restored to its 1920s look, and it's remarkable to reflect on how modest the man's background was compared to the grandeur of the dreams he realized. The city of Coral Gables took its name from this house. The stone was quarried from what is now the Venetian Pool. 🗺 *907 Coral Way • 305-460-5361 • House 1–4pm Wed & Sun; grounds, 8am–sunset daily • Adm to house, gardens free*

10 Coconut Grove Playhouse
In a reversal of the usual story, this period Mediterranean-Revival building, in the Spanish Rococo style, was built in 1926 as a movie house and later converted to a theater *(see p38)*.

Left **Midori Gallery** Right **Books and Books**

Boutiques

Modernism Gallery
One of the country's top dealers in ultracool furniture, lighting fixtures, and accessories, including Art Deco. ⊗ *1622 Ponce de León Blvd at Mendoza Ave, Coral Gables*

Midori Gallery
Exquisite, museum-quality Chinese and Japanese ceramics, lacquers and ivories, some as old as the Eastern Han Dynasty, 25–220 AD. Other sublime pieces date from the Sung Dynasty, about 1,000 years ago. ⊗ *3168 Commodore Plaza, Coconut Grove*

Palm Produce Resortwear
Florida lifestyle clothing means loose and colorful, natural fabrics, and somewhat frivolous designs for both men and women. ⊗ *3390 Mary Street, Streets of Mayfair, Coconut Grove*

French Connection
The only French Connection shop in Florida, featuring the young, trendy, sophisticated, and somewhat cheeky British styles. ⊗ *Streets of Mayfair, Coconut Grove*

Book and Books
Just a block off the Miracle Mile is this wonderful bookshop specializing in the arts and literature, as well as books on Florida. There's a great café, frequent poetry readings, and book signings. Upstairs you'll find a rare books room, which is also a photo gallery. ⊗ *265 Aragon Ave, Coral Gables*

White House
A rarified collection of women's fashion, all of it white. Elegant, sequined evening gowns, smart suits, peignoirs, and underthings. Prices suit the quality of the fabrics and workmanship. ⊗ *3015 Grand Ave, CocoWalk*

Expertees Golf Shop
With all the very latest lines of clubs and putters, and accessories, this shop also offers a state-of-the-art computerized swing analysis, shaft lab, club fitting center, and lessons for beginners and low handicappers. ⊗ *2329 Coral Way*

Hibiscus Hill
A unique gift shop with a captivating range of handmade objects: elaborate jewelry, hand-blown glass, and imported *objets*, all with a distinctly fabulous air. Fabulous prices, too, for the most part. ⊗ *Streets of Mayfair, 2911 Grand Ave, Coconut Grove*

Out of Africa
The sound of African drums fills the air, and hand-carved wooden figures and masks, and silver jewelry fill the space. ⊗ *Streets of Mayfair, 2911 Grand Ave, Coconut Grove*

Borders
Not just a delightfully complete bookstore, but also a snack and coffee bar, and just a great place to hang out. ⊗ *3390 Mary St at Grand Ave, Coconut Grove*

Price Categories

For a three-course meal for one with half a bottle of wine (or equivalent meal), taxes, and extra charges.

$	under $20
$$	$20–$40
$$$	$40–$55
$$$$	$55–$80
$$$$$	over $80

Left **Norman's** Right **The Cheesecake Factory**

🔟 Trendy Restaurants

1 Norman's
Norman Van Aiken is the country's chief protagonist of New World fusion cuisine. Experience opulent aspects of tuna, foie gras, fish, seafood, and even simple salad greens that you never knew existed. ◎ *21 Almeria Ave, Coral Gables • 305-446-6767 • $$$$$*

2 Restaurant Place St. Michel
A romantic spot, capturing the feel of Paris. Every bite is a thrill to the palate, although it is hardly French, leaning more to the Caribbean. Grilled fish with plantains and salsa, for example. ◎ *Hotel Place St. Michel. 162 Alcazar Ave, Coral Gables • 305-446-6572 • $$$$*

3 Orsini
Adventurous dishes such as pan-seared foie gras with pears and sweet Japanese wine reduction make intriguing counterpoints to more standard fare, such as grilled salmon. ◎ *2901 Florida Ave, Coconut Grove • 305-774-6397 • $$$*

4 Monty's Stone Crab Seafood House and Raw Bar
A vast dining room in an old airplane hangar. Try the Jamaican jerk spiced fish, or just go for the excellent peel-and-eat shrimp and raw oysters. It's a Miami institution. ◎ *2550 Bayshore Drive, Coconut Grove • 305-858-1431 • $$$$*

5 Giralda Café
The 1,000-year-old traditions of Peruvian cookery – e.g. fried yucca with *huancaina* sauce, fish and shrimp cevíche, and beef stew in cilantro (coriander) sauce. ◎ *254 Giralda Ave, Coral Gables • 305-448-6064 • $$*

6 Baleen
Fresh oysters shucked at your table, the best lobster bisque on Biscayne Bay, oak-smoked diver scallops, and Asian bouillabaisse are some of the treats. ◎ *4 Grove Isle Drive, Coconut Grove • 305-857-5007 • $$$$$*

7 The Cheesecake Factory
One of six in South Florida, serving everything from pot stickers to shepherd's pie, and, of course, at least 36 types of cheesecake. ◎ *3015 Grand Ave, CocoWalk • 305-447-9898 • $$*

8 Anokha Fine Indian Cuisine
Tandoori a specialty, and side dishes featuring homemade paneer cheese. ◎ *3195 Commodore Plaza, Coconut Grove • (786) 552-1030 • $$$*

9 Titanic Brewing Company
Lift a pint of homemade brew and sample crawfish or calamari snacks. ◎ *5813 Ponce de Leon Blvd, Coral Gables • 305-667-2537 • $*

10 Café Tu Tu Tango
"Food for the starving artist" is their by-line, and, indeed, artists and their works are all over the place. Wonderful light fare, such as seared sashimi tuna salad, and crispy shrimp brochettes. ◎ *CocoWalk • 305-529-2222 • $$*

> **Note:** Unless otherwise stated, all restaurants have disabled access, accept credit cards, and serve vegetarian meals

Left **Charles Deering Estate** Right **Coral Castle**

South of Coconut Grove

HEADING SOUTH FROM MIAMI'S MAIN EVENTS, *once you get past the dull, nondescript suburbs, you enter vast tracts of citrus groves and tropical nurseries. The general mood changes, too – a bit backwoodsy, a bit Old South. Though sometimes gruff, the people here are friendly enough, and there are plenty of shopping opportunities, parks, gardens, zoos, and museums. You'll notice that the natural landscape looks a bit mauled – the area took the full brunt of Hurricane Andrew's muscle in 1992 and is still recovering.*

Left **Coral Castle sculpture** Right **Fairchild Tropical Garden**

🔟 Sights

1. Fairchild Tropical Garden
2. Charles Deering Estate
3. Miami Metrozoo
4. Monkey Jungle
5. Coral Castle
6. Wings Over Miami
7. Gold Coast Railroad Museum
8. Biscayne National Underwater Park
9. Florida International University Art Museum
10. Fruit & Spice Park

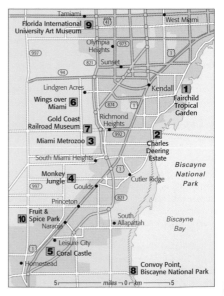

1 Fairchild Tropical Garden

This dizzyingly beautiful tropical paradise was established in 1938 and serves also as a botanical research institute. Around a series of man-made lakes stands one of the largest collections of palm trees in the world (550 of the 2,500 known species), as well as countless other wonderful trees and plants. During a 40-minute tram tour,

Miami Metrozoo

guides describe how plants are used in the manufacture of everything from Chanel No. 5 to golf balls. Allow another two hours to explore on your own. ✆ 10901 Old Cutler Rd • Map G4 • 305-667-1651 • www.ftg.org • 9:30am–4:30pm daily • Adm

2 Charles Deering Estate

Right on Biscayne Bay, the estate contains two significant architectural works: Richmond Cottage, built in 1896 as the area's first inn, and a large Mediterranean-Revival "Stone House," built in 1922. You can also visit what is thought to be a Pre-Columbian burial site and a fascinating fossil pit. ✆ 16701 SW 72nd Ave, at SW 167th St & Old Cutler Rd • Map F4 • 305-235-1668 • 10am–4pm daily • Adm

3 Miami Metrozoo

The zoo works a great deal with endangered species. Zookeepers give talks at feeding times. ✆ 12400 SW 152 St • Map E4 • 305-251-0400 • www.miamimetro zoo.com • Adm

4 Monkey Jungle

This endearing attraction is still run by the family that founded it in 1933 to study the behavior of primates. Many of the smaller monkeys roam wild while you walk through caged walkways; the gorillas, orangutans, spider monkeys, and gibbons are kept in conventional cages. There are regular demonstrations of the capabilities of macaques, chimpanzees, and other human cousins. ✆ 14805 SW 216th St, Cutler Ridge • Map F5 • 305-235-1611 • www.monkey jungle.com • 9:30am–5pm • Adm

5 Coral Castle

A castle it isn't, but a conundrum it certainly is. From 1920 to 1940, Latvian immigrant Edward Leedskalnin built this mysterious pile as a Valentine to the girl back home, who had jilted him in 1913. No one knows how he single-handedly quarried and transported the 1,100 tons of tough coral rock, carved all the enormous chunks into monumental shapes, and set them all into place so flawlessly. One nine-ton gate is so exquisitely balanced that it opens with the pressure of your little finger. ✆ 28655 South Dixie Hwy • Map E6 • 305-248-6345 • www.coral castle.com • 9am–7pm daily • Adm

For a suggested day's itinerary incorporating the Deering Estate See p109

Coral Castle

6 Wings Over Miami

This military and classic aircraft museum acts as a tribute to early inventors, veterans, and aviators, some of whom set world records with the planes on display here. Exhibits include early biplanes and an all-plywood DeHavilland. ◎ *Tamiami Airport, 14710 SW 128th St at SW 147th Ave, South Dade • Map E4 • 305-233-5197*
• *www.wingsovermiami.com*
• *10am–5:30pm Thu–Sun • Adm*

7 Gold Coast Railroad Museum

The museum was started in 1957, by a group of Miamians who were trying to save threatened pieces of Florida history. Some of the earliest items in the collection are the "Ferdinand Magellan," a private railroad car built for President Franklin Roosevelt; the FEC engine that pulled a rescue train out from Marathon after the 1935 hurricane; and the 113 locomotive built in 1913. The Edwin Link is a small-gauge children's railroad. ◎ *12450 SW 152nd St • Map F4 • 888-608-7246*
• *www.goldcoast-railroad.org • 11am–3pm daily, to 4pm on weekends • Adm*

8 Biscayne National Underwater Park

Biscayne National Underwater Park is 95 percent water, therefore most visitors enter it

Hurricane Country

One in ten of the North Atlantic hurricanes hits Florida, which means an average of one big storm every two years. On August 24, 1992, Hurricane Andrew was one such storm, measuring 4 on the Saffir-Simpson Scale. The worst is a 5, like the one that hit the Keys in 1935, destroying the Flagler bridge.

by private boat. Otherwise, the Dante Fascell Visitor Center at Convoy Point is the only place in the national park you can drive to and, from there, you have several boating options. The concession offers canoe rentals, glass-bottom boat tours, snorkel trips, scuba trips, and transportation to the island for campers. There's also a picturesque boardwalk that takes you along the shoreline out to the rock jetty beside the boat channel heading to the bay.
◎ *SW 328th St (North Canal Drive)*
• *Map D5 • 305-230-7275*
• *www.nps.gov/bisc • 8:30am–5pm daily*

Gold Coast Railroad Museum

9 Florida International University Art Museum

The museum specializes in Latin American and 20th-century American art and presents six to eight major

Dubuffet exhibit, University Museum

exhibitions each year. The Martin Z. Margulies Sculpture Park displays 69 works in a variety of media distributed throughout the 26.5 acres of the FIU campus – a wonderfully rich and important representation of modern work. It is recognized nationally as one of the world's great collections of sculpture and the largest on a university campus. It includes major pieces by Dubuffet, Miro, Nevelson, Calder, Noguchi, and Serra. ✪ University Park, PC 110 • Map F3 • 305-348-2890 • 10am–9pm Mon, 10am–5pm Tue–Fri, noon–4pm Sat & Sun • 1-hr tours throughout year • Free

10 Fruit & Spice Park

This 30-acre (12-ha) tropical botanical park is devoted to exotic plants, such as citrus fruits, grapes, bananas, herbs, spices, nuts, and bamboo. It forms a unique attraction in the United States – after all, South Florida's tropical climate is found nowhere else in the US. The astonishing number of varieties on display include a selection of poisonous species and hundreds of bamboo and banana varieties. A wonderful store enables you to stock up your cupboards with many unusual fruit products. ✪ 24801 Redland Road (SW 187th Ave), Homestead • Map E6 • 305-247-5727 • 10am–5pm daily • Adm/guided tours

Deering Estate Walk

Morning

🕐 To get to the **Charles Deering Estate** (see p107), drive south from Miami on Hwy 1 (also called the Dixie Hwy) and turn left on SW 168th St. Follow it until it deadends at the Estate on SW 72nd Ave.

A full tour of the grounds will take 3–4 hours. Follow the Entrance Trail to begin, and as you emerge from the mangroves you will encounter a splendid vista of Biscayne Bay. Note the water level marker, showing the inundation caused by Hurricane Andrew.

Richmond Cottage, the original structure here, was built as an inn in 1896. It was destroyed by Andrew in 1992, but has since been replicated. The elegant Stone House next door contains bronze and copper doors, portraits of the Deering family, a celebrated wine cellar, and more besides.

Head over to the Carriage House, where you can see a vintage gas pump. If you have time, take the Main Nature Trail, which crosses a handsome coral rock bridge, built in 1918. Finally, walk out through the historic Main Entrance, with its coral rock pillars and wood and iron gates.

Afternoon

Picnicking on the grounds is a possibility, and some facilities are provided. Or, for an elegant lunch, head south to the **Cauley Square Tea Room** (see p111). To make a full day's outing, head farther south along Hwy 1 to the eccentric **Coral Castle** (see p107).

Left **Maddie's World exterior** Right **Maddie's World interior**

Regional Souvenir Shops

1 Pink Umbrella Gallery
Hand-painted furniture and all sorts of accessories, large and small, for indoors or out, such as charming birdhouses. ◈ Cauley Square, 22400 Old Dixie Highway, Goulds

2 Maddie's World
Crystals, jewelry, and gifts, including natural cosmetics and fragrances, and lush silk paintings. ◈ Cauley Square

3 Today's Collectibles
You'll have to step over the dogs as you enter from the front porch. Inside you'll find Tiffany-style lamps, marcasite and antique jewelry, antique furniture, and collectibles. ◈ Cauley Square, 12360 SW 224 St

4 Studio G Designs
A range of handicrafts made by local artists; it's also a year-round Christmas store. ◈ Cauley Square, 12345 SW 224 St

5 Tropical Attitudes Hawaii
Bright and breezy natural-fiber resort wear is made here, all of it original design. The designer will make things to order. ◈ Cauley Square, 12365 SW 224 St

6 The Aviary
Here's the place for you if you've finally decided you must sport a macaw or cockatoo on your shoulder. Plus, you can buy your new pet a Tiki Hut cage and all the seed and accoutrements it will need for a joyous, talkative life as your companion. A wonderful place to visit, laid out like a tropical garden. ◈ 22707 South Dixie Hwy • www.aviarybirdshop.com

7 Homestead Antique Mall
A pleasant little mall in downtown Homestead. Spaces, to the left as you enter, and Found Treasures, toward the end on the right, are very appealing. A classic shell-encrusted clock or mirror, for example, is utterly characteristic of regional Florida culture. ◈ 115 N Krome Ave, Homestead

8 Goneteaking Antiques
One of the more inviting of Homestead's 20-odd antiques shops, at least half of which are on Krome Avenue, the town's main street. Snoop here for fine antiques, old clocks, Victorian bric-a-brac, Depression glass, pottery, vintage linens, jewelry, etc. ◈ 107 Krome Ave, Homestead

9 ArtSouth
Local artists live and work here, giving classes as well as selling their work. ◈ 240 N Krome Ave, Homestead

10 Ochun Oggún Botánica
Seems that every little South Florida community has at least one Botánica (Cuban spiritual store). Stop by to pick up some extra True Love Spice or an amulet of Changò, a Yoruba god. ◈ 864 N Krome Ave, Homestead

You'll recognize Cauley Square from Highway 1 as the quaint, Spanish-style hacienda off to the right as you head south

O'Caseys Restaurant and Irish Pub

🔟 Regional Eateries

1 Red Fish Grill
One of Miami's most romantic spots, nestled amid the tropical magic of Matheson Hammock Park. Great, freshly caught fish, prepared lovingly with a Caribbean flair, and a range of other dishes. 🚫 9610 Old Cutler Rd • 305-668-9975 • $$$

Sign for the Red Fish Grill

2 La Porteña
Traditional Argentine *parrillada*, but also things like ostrich, caviar crêpes stuffed with mascarpone and Manchego cheeses, and savory mussels sautéed with roasted garlic. 🚫 8520 SW 8th St • 305-263-5808 • $$$

3 O'Casey's Restaurant and Irish Pub
Shepherd's pie, grilled meat, fish, and chicken, and, of course, an array of Irish brews. A refreshing departure from all the haute cuisine and Latino-Caribbean influences. 🚫 11415 S. Dixie Hwy, Pinecrest • 305-256-2667 • $$

4 Tropical Chinese
The food is Chinese and excellent, the setting tropical, big, and busy. Expect abalone, shrimp with garlic and spinach in clay pots, seafood tofu soup, and more. 🚫 7991 Bird Rd • 305-262-7576 • $$$

5 Trattoria Sole
The baby spinach salad with raisins and pinenuts works well, as does the polenta with wild boar sausage. 🚫 5894 Sunset Dr • 305-666-9392 • $$$

6 Guadalajara
Original, home-cooked Mexican fare in a locale full of character. The portions are huge, so just an appetizer might do. Try dipping a warm tortilla in a *queso fundido* (cheese fondue). 🚫 8461 SW 132nd St, Pinecrest • 786-242-4444 • $

7 Café de las Artes Restaurant and Steakhouse
Italian-Argentine-with-a-dash-of-Cuban place with *empanadas*: pies stuffed with spinach, chicken, or ham and cheese. 🚫 6500 SW 40th St (Bird Road) • 305-661-3888 • $$

8 Grappa
Cozy Italian with a full South Florida-inspired menu. Finish off with the eponymous firewater – chilled grappa. 🚫 5837 Sunset Dr • 305-668-9119 • $$$

9 Sushi Maki
Good sushi at reasonable prices. The volcano roll is a creamy, multi-fish treat, or choose from 30 other creative rolls. 🚫 5812 Sunset Dr • 305-667-7677 • $

10 Cauley Square Tea Room
A light and lacy setting in a period cottage. Order hot crab-meat au gratin, a large tuna-nut salad, or a shrimp platter. 🚫 12310 SW 224th St • 305-258-0044 • $

Note: *Unless otherwise stated, all restaurants have disabled access, accept credit cards, and serve vegetarian meals*

Left **Crowd at Key West** Center **Duval Street, Key West** Right **Dolphin Research Center**

The Keys

THE FLORIDA KEYS ARE A STRING OF WILD, *variegated gems hung in a necklace of liquid turquoise.* These islands still have abundant wildlife, including unique flora and fauna, as evidenced by all the parks and family attractions focusing on encounters with nature. Even so, at least 20 different species of Keys plant and animal life are endangered or threatened. This is a place for outdoor activities: water sports of all kinds, sportfishing, and hiking through the nature preserves and virgin tropical forests. Along the only route (US 1) that takes you from the mainland all the way out to Key West, you'll find everything from plush resorts to roadside stands selling home-grown produce.

🔟 Sights

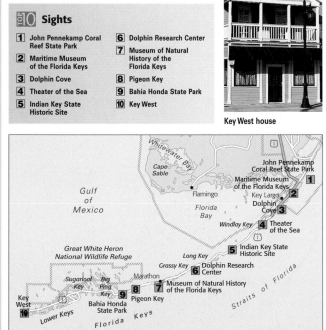

1. John Pennekamp Coral Reef State Park
2. Maritime Museum of the Florida Keys
3. Dolphin Cove
4. Theater of the Sea
5. Indian Key State Historic Site
6. Dolphin Research Center
7. Museum of Natural History of the Florida Keys
8. Pigeon Key
9. Bahia Honda State Park
10. Key West

Key West house

Previous pages **Harbor at Key West**

Jetty, John Pennekamp Park

John Pennekamp Coral Reef State Park

The park is best known for its fabulous underwater reaches, providing an unforgettable glimpse of coral reef life. You can also rent canoes, dinghies, or motorboats, as well as snorkeling and scuba gear, or choose a glass-bottom boat ride. Most destinations are actually located in the neighboring Florida Keys (Key Largo) National Marine Sanctuary. The shallow waters of White Bank Dry Rocks is especially good for snorkeling, as well as nearby Molasses Reef. At Key Largo Dry Rocks, the Christ of the Deep, a submerged statue, is popular for underwater photos. ☜ *MM 102.5 oceanside • Map D5 • 305-451-1202 • 8am–sunset daily • Adm*

Maritime Museum of the Florida Keys

Displays about coral reefs and related themes. The exploits of various pirates are recounted, and exhibits include treasures recovered over the years. Many items on display were

Coral, John Pennekamp Park

pulled up from the remains of the ship Concepción, which sank in a hurricane in 1715. ☜ *MM 102 • Map C5 • 305-451-6444*

Dolphin Cove

This marine environment research center, set on a lagoon, will literally let you swim with the dolphins – for a high fee. You can go in as a non-swimming observer for a lot less money. Other programs include guided kayaking and snorkeling tours, back country eco-tours, and crocodile tours. By contrast, there's also a romantic champagne Sunset Cruise on the placid waters of Florida Bay. ☜ *MM 101.9 Bayside • Map C5 • 305-451-4060 • 8am–5pm daily • Dolphin swim sessions at 9am, 1pm and 3:30pm Sat & Sun only • Adm • www.dolphinscove.com*

Theater of the Sea

Did you know that dolphins feel like wet inner tubes and stingrays like Jello (gelatin)? After a visit here, you'd have first hand experience. This is the world's second-oldest (since 1946) marine mammal facility and offers a wide variety of shows and programs. There are dolphin and sea lion shows or, if you prefer, you can swim with them here, too. For a big fee, "Swim With the Dolphins" guarantees hugs, dorsal tows, and smooches. "Swim With the Sea Lions" includes flipper tows and hugs, too. "Swim With the Stingrays" is the least expensive – a snorkeling visit to the domain of the gentle creatures. ☜ *MM 84.5 oceanside • Map C5 • 305-664-2431 • www.theaterofthesea.com • 9:30am–4pm daily • Adm*

Left **Dolphin Research Center** Right **Dolphins**

5 Indian Key State Historic Site

Tiny Indian Key has a surprising amount of history for its size (10.5 acres/4.25ha). An ancient Native American site, it was settled in 1831 by Captain J. Houseman, an opportunistic wrecker. A small community flourished under his autocratic rule, but in 1840 Seminoles attacked, killing the settlers. The Key was abandoned, and today only the outlines of the village remain, overgrown by vegetation impressive for both its variety and rampant growth. These are the descendants of plants belonging to Dr. Henry Perrine, a botanist who was killed in the raid. An observation tower provides splendid views. ◈ *MM 78.5 ocean-side • Map C5 • 305-664-9814 for ferry service*
• Sunrise–sunset daily

6 Dolphin Research Center

A not-for-profit concern, whose main function is to research dolphin behavior and provide a rest home for sick and injured dolphins, or those worn out from theme-park living. There are exhibits, regularly scheduled lagoon-side walking tours, and special programs featuring the Atlantic bottlenose dolphins. "Dolphin Encounter" lets you swim and interact with the creatures. Some programs

Shell, Museum of Natural History

The Keys: Myth and Magic

The very name conjures up visions of windswept seascapes and wild goings-on: Humphrey Bogart and Lauren Bacall in the classic melodrama, *Key Largo*; some of the greatest American writers (Ernest Hemingway, Tennessee Williams, et al.) finding their respective muses where the US meets the Caribbean; and a free, unfettered lifestyle that seems too good to be true.

have age or height restrictions and require 30-day advance reservations. ◈ *MM 59 bayside • Map C6 • 305-289-0002 • www. dolphins.org • 9am–4pm daily • Adm*

7 Museum of Natural History of the Florida Keys

You can see a 600-year-old dugout canoe, remnants of pirate ships, a simulated coral reef cave, and the Bellarmine jug (circa 1580), a shipwreck artifact in almost perfect condition. There's also the Florida Keys Children's Museum and Marathon Wild Bird Center. ◈ *MM 50.5 bayside • Map B6 • 305-743-9100 • 9am–5pm Mon–Sat, noon–5pm Sun • Adm*

8 Pigeon Key

This was originally the site of the work camp for those who built Henry M. Flagler's Overseas Railroad Bridge, described as the

Bahia Honda State Park

eighth wonder of the world when it was completed in 1912. A marine research foundation is housed in the old buildings. To get to the island, you can walk or take the shuttle, which uses a section of the original bridge.
⊘ *Shuttle depot at MM 47 oceanside • Map B6 • 305-289-0025 • www.pigeon key.org • 9am-5pm daily • Adm*

9 Bahia Honda State Park
This protected area boasts the finest beaches in all the Keys – and is often voted among the best in the US. Brilliantly white sand is backed by dense, tropical forest crossed by a number of nature trails. ⊘ *Bahia Honda Key, Milemarker 37 oceanside • Map B6 • 305-872-2353 • Adm*

10 Key West
Rich in history and breath-taking beauty, the self-styled Conch (pronounced "conk") Republic seems truly a world apart from the rest of the US *(see pp26–7)*.

Duval Street, Key West

A Day's Walk on Key West

Morning

Begin at about 10am. Start at the Southermost Point in the continental US, over-looking the Atlantic at the intersection of Whitehead and South Streets, where the marker informs you that Cuba is only 90 miles (144 km) away. Then head up Whitehead to the **Lighthouse Museum** and climb its 88 steps for a great overview of the island and beyond.

Next stop is **Hemingway House**, at 907; here you can take in a nostalgic trip through the writer's life as a Conch. Then move on to the **Green Parrot Bar**, at 601 Whitehead, to admire its age-old funkiness and have a drink before lunch. From here, head over to Duval Street, to **Mangoes Restaurant**, at 700, for a great lunch and equally stellar people-watching.

Afternoon

Afterwards, take a look at the Spanish Colonial façade of the **San Carlos Opera House**, and, on the next block up, the stained-glass windows of **St. Paul's Episcopal Church**. At 322, pay a visit to the **Wreckers' Museum**.

Now things might get very "Key West," as you climb to the third floor of The Bull at 224 to find **The Garden of Eden** and see who's sunning themselves in this clothing-optional bar.

Farther along, stop at his-toric **Sloppy Joe's** bar. By now, it should be time for the famous sunset celebra-tion, so head to Mallory Square and add your posi-tive energy to the festivities!

Left **Mangrove, Key Largo Hammocks State Botanical Site** Right **Bahia Honda**

Nature Preserves

1 Key Largo Hammocks State Botanical Site

The largest remaining stand of tropical West Indian hardwood and mangrove is a refuge for protected indigenous flora and fauna. ✎ *1 mile N of US 1, on Route 905, oceanside • 305-451-1202 • 8am–5pm daily, guided tours 10am Thu & Sun • Free*

2 John Pennekamp Coral Reef State Park

Most famous for its stunning offshore coral reef, where snorkeling, scuba diving, and glass-bottom boat rides are great favorites *(see p115)*.

3 Florida Keys Wild Bird Rehabilitation Center

A safe haven for recovering Keys birds of all types. Healed ones are set free, if they like. ✎ *MM 93.6, bayside • 305-852-4486 • Sunrise–sunset daily • Donation*

4 Windley Key Fossil Reef State Geological Site

Nature displays in the center, and trails into the railroad's old quarries, where you can see fossilized brain coral and sea ferns. ✎ *MM 85.5 bayside • 305-664-2540 • 8am–5pm Thu–Mon • Adm*

5 Lignumvitae Key State Botanical Site

Access is by boat only to this virgin hardwood forest home and gardens built by William Matheson. Call the Long Key Recreation Area to arrange a tour. ✎ *MM 78.5 bayside • 305-664-9814 for ferry*

6 Long Key State Park

Features include a boardwalk through a mangrove swamp next to a lagoon where you can see water birds. Snorkeling is good in the shallow waters off the beach. ✎ *MM 67.5 oceanside • 305-664-4815 • 8am–sunset daily • Adm*

7 Crane Point Hammock Museums and Nature Center

Walk the nature trails to Florida Bay and check out the Museum of Natural History of the Florida Keys *(see p116)* and the Adderly Town Historic Site. ✎ *MM 50 bayside • 305-743-9100 • 9am–5pm Mon-Sat, noon–5pm Sun • Adm*

8 Bahia Honda State Recreation Area

Very heavily forested, with great nature trails. Fascinating snorkeling, too *(see p117)*.

9 National Key Deer Refuge

Fewer than 50 of these diminutive creatures were left until this refuge was established in 1957. Now there are estimated to be about 800. Drive very slowly. ✎ *MM 30.5 bayside • 305-872-0774 • Sunrise–sunset daily • Free*

10 Florida Keys National Marine Sanctuary

Looe Key Reef is one of the Keys' most spectacular coral reefs and is great for snorkeling and diving. Call for information about boat trips to the best spots. ✎ *MM 27.5 oceanside • 305-292-0311*

Left **Egrets and the rare roseate spoonbill** Right **Endangered American crocodiles**

Plants and Animals in the Keys

1 Key Deer
The diminutive Key deer (max. 32 in/81 cm tall) are found primarily on Big Pine and No Name keys. Docile and endearing, these tiny animals have returned from the brink of extinction in the last 40 years.

2 Coral
Although it appears to be insensate rock, coral is actually a living organism, and a very fragile one at that, easily damaged by the slightest touch.

3 Gumbo Limbo Tree
This unmistakable tree is found all over the Keys – called the "tourist tree" because its bark is red and peeling.

4 Palms
Although only a few species are natives – the royal palm, the sabal palm, the saw palmetto, and the thatch palm – a huge range of imported palms now adorn the islands.

5 Sea Turtles
These good-natured, long-lived creatures come in a wide variety of shapes and sizes. From the largest to the smallest they are the leatherback, the loggerhead, the green, the hawksbill, and the Ridley turtles.

6 Herons
These elegant birds include the great blue heron (white phase, too), the little blue heron, the tri-colored heron, the green-backed heron, and the black-crowned night heron.

7 Egrets
Similar to herons are the great egret, the snowy egret (distinguishable by its black legs and yellow feet), and the reddish egret.

8 White Ibis
Recognizable for its long, down-curving beak, this medium-sized white bird was sacred to the Egyptians.

9 Double-Crested Cormorant
Notable for its S-curved neck, distinctive beak, and spectacular diving skills, this is one of the most fascinating of Keys birds.

Heron in the Keys

10 Other Endangered Species
These include the American crocodile, the Key Largo wood rat and cotton mouse, Schaus swallowtail butterfly, and roseate spoonbill, all of which have either been hunted to near extinction or lost their habitats due to human encroachment.

Left **Sign for a dive center in the Keys** Center **Parasailing** Right **Sailing**

🔟 Sports Activities in the Keys

1 Swimming
Some of the best beaches in the world are found in the Keys. Don't worry if the ocean temperature happens to fall below the usual 79°F (26°C) – most hotels have heated swimming pools.

2 Snorkeling and Scuba Diving
Since the Keys are almost entirely surrounded by America's largest living coral reef, the underwater world is one of the main treats the area has to offer.

3 Fishing
Deep-sea fishermen find the Keys to be paradise. With the Gulf Stream nearby, these waters offer the most varied fishing imaginable. Boat trips are easy to come by; try the Key West Fishing Club. ◎ *Fishing Club 305-294-3618 • www.keywestfishingclub.com*

4 Windsurfing
With prevailing winds and calm, shallow waters that remain so for miles out to sea, the Keys are windsurfing perfection. Most moderately busy beaches up and down the islands have shops that rent all the necessary equipment.

5 Parasailing
As close to growing wings as you can get, parasailing in the Keys is easy, safe, and unforgettable. Many small companies offer the experience, such as Sebago, on the Key West Bight. ◎ *Sebago 305-292-2411*

6 Bicycling
There is no doubt that bicycling is one of the best ways to see the Keys. The roads are fairly bike-friendly, especially in Key West, and bicycle rentals are readily available.

7 Boating and Sailing
The many dozens of marinas in the Keys are full of companies ready to rent you whatever kind of boat you would like – or to take you out, if you prefer.

8 Water-skiing and Jet-skiing
These more intense ways of enjoying the Keys waters are available wherever there's a marina, especially, of course in Key West and other developed tourist areas. Island Water Sport is one of the companies offering jetskis. ◎ *Island Water Sport 305-296-1754*

9 Golf
Golf courses are not as ubiquitous in the Keys as in the rest of Florida, but there are several good ones, for example on Marathon Key at MM 53.5 oceanside or a more expensive course on Key West.

10 Tennis
Good tennis clubs can be found on just about every developed Key – on Islamorada at MM 76.8 bayside, Marathon at MM 53.5 oceanside, on Key West, of course, and elsewhere.

For more on the beaches and watersports in the Keys and around Miami **See pp30–35**

Left **The Seven-Mile Bridge** Right **Hemingway lookalikes during Hemingway Days**

🔟 Special Tours and Events

1 Conch Tour Train
Key West's train tour is a must-do for first-time visitors. It gives an invaluable overview of the place and all sorts of insights into its history and culture.

2 Dry Tortugas
Take a plane or ferry to this totally undeveloped collection of islands, where the snorkeling is unbeatable *(see pp32 & 129)*.

3 Old Town Ghost Walk
A lantern-lit evening stroll through the mysterious streets of Key's West's Old Town allows you to discover a haunted island. *Tours depart each evening from the Holiday Inn La Concha Hotel, 450 Duval St*

4 Goombay Celebration
A celebration of Island culture and life, with the emphasis on great music. Held in mid-October, it usually merges with the Fantasy Fest (below). *Bahama Village, Key West • 305-295-3851*

5 Fantasy Fest
Held on Key West in October, for at least ten days leading up to and including Halloween, this is the festival with the most fun, positive atmosphere the US has to offer *(see p40)*.

6 Cuban American Heritage Festival
In June, Key West remembers its rich Cuban heritage and celebrates with ethnic foods, terrific music, and dancing in the streets of the island. *305-295-9665*

7 Old Island Days
This is a crafts show held in late January, but also an excuse for "Conchs" to celebrate being themselves – something they're always ready to do in Key West. *305-294-1241*

8 Annual Conch-Blowing Contest
Late March is when this traditional means of musical expression – or noise-making in less skilled cases – fills the air over Key West. Expect anything from poetic foghorn-like sounds to pathetic blats. It's great fun for children. *305-7294-9501*

9 Seven-Mile Bridge Run
In mid- to late April, enthusiastic runners honor the bridge that joined all the Keys together by conquering it with their own two feet. *Marathon Key • 305-743-5417*

10 Hemingway Days
Since it's held in the middle of the low season, the third week of July (Hemingway's birthday was July 21st), this party is mainly for the "Conchs." Consequently, it seems to be the celebration most loved by the locals. Hemingway lookalikes help lead the celebrations and tributes to the island's most famous writer. *305-294-1136*

 For more information on special tours and events in the Keys, contact the Key West Vistor Center on 1-800-527-8539

Left **Archaeo** Right **Key West Hand Print**

TOP 10 Island Shopping

1 The Gallery at Kona Kai Resort

Impressive selection of international artwork, including painting (Sobran and Magni), sculpture (Pollès bronzes), and stunning Keys nature photography. ❧ *MM 97.8 bayside, 97802 Overseas Highway (US 1) • www.konakairesort.com*

2 Treasure Village

An inviting complex, notable for the giant lobster sculpture outside and a real parrot in the central courtyard, which houses crafts and specialty shops. ❧ *MM 86.7 oceanside, 86729 Old Highway (US 1) • www.hellokeys.com*

3 Archeo

Rare African masks and wood carvings, combined with dozens of stunning Persian rugs, make this shop one of the most beautiful in town. ❧ *1208 Duval St, Key West • www.archeogallery.com*

4 Environmental Circus

"Let the flowers grow and the music flow." This delirious shop (est. 1970) is like entering a time warp and returning to the dippy days of hippie hedonism. Headshop apparatus, weird comics, and flower-child fashions, too. ❧ *518 Duval Street, Key West*

5 Key West Aloe

A company that has made their own all-natural products right here since 1971, without any animal testing. ❧ *524 Front Street, Key West • www.keywestaloe.com*

6 Cuba! Cuba!

Since Key West is closer to Cuba than to the Florida mainland, it makes sense to find a Cuban crafts shop here, despite the official embargo. Items include handmade boxes, dolls, and paintings. ❧ *814 Duval Street, Key West • www.cubacubastore.com*

7 Key West Hand Print

In one of the few brick buildings that survived the great fire of 1886, this huge store sells hand-printed fabrics and fashions. ❧ *201 Simonton St, Key West • www.keywestfashions.com*

8 Peppers of Key West

A wonderful range of spicy sauces for all purposes – from barbecuing to killing off your enemies. ❧ *602 Greene Street, Key West • www.peppersofkeywest.com*

9 Grand Vin

Great wines from around the world at good prices, and the chance to try many of them by the glass. Sit out on the porch and watch the life on the street. ❧ *1107 Duval Street, Key West*

10 Conch Republic Cigar Factory

"Savor the flavor of paradise" is their motto, and this old factory probably does, in fact, turn out the next best thing to a genuine Cuban stogie. Prices range from $3 to $10.75 for a single cigar. ❧ *512 Greene Street, Key West • www.conch-cigars.com*

Left **Bourbon Street** Center **La-Te-Da** Right **Graffiti**

🔟 Gay and Lesbian Venues

1 Gay and Lesbian Community Center, Key West
There's always plenty of information here for the taking, as well as occasional events.

2 Bourbon Street Complex
Included here are the popular Bourbon Street Pub, the 801 Bourbon Bar, 1 Saloon, Magnolia's and Pizza Joe's, and The New Orleans House, a gay guesthouse. 801 features drag shows every night in the upstairs bar. 🔊 *722-801 Duval Street, Key West*

3 Atlantic Shores Resort
Right on the water, with its own deck, pool, and pier, they've been sponsoring a Tea Dance every Sunday evening for over 20 years. Clothing always optional. Open to participants of all sexual inclinations. 🔊 *511 South Street, Key West • 305-296-2491*

4 La-Te-Da
More upscale than the other venues, and with its own excellent restaurant, too, this is a popular gay and lesbian spot of long-standing. "Guys as Dolls" and other acts in the Crystal Room Cabaret every night. 🔊 *1125 Duval Street, Key West • 305-296-6706*

5 KWEST
Multi-bar complex featuring a nightly drag show, men dancing for men, a leather bar and shop, and occasional theme nights. 🔊 *771 Duval St, Key West • 305-292-8500*

6 Graffiti
Trendy and pricey styles designed with the young gay male in mind. Most of the fashions are understated, but there's also a good selection of flash to suit the mood of this sybaritic island. 🔊 *701 Duval Street, Key West*

7 In Touch
Lots of amusing erotica, cards, sexy clothing, toys, and other same-sex fun stuff for both gay men and lesbians. 🔊 *715 Duval Street, Key West*

8 Xposure
Rather extreme club wear for men – animal prints, imitation snakeskin, day-glow plastic – at not so extreme prices. 🔊 *608 Greene St, Key West*

9 Leatherotica
The smell of leather wafts your way as soon as you enter, and all of it's black, with stainless steel studs. You can watch the craftsman at his work table, shaping the leather into various hard-wearing items.
🔊 *405B Petronia Street, Key West*
• *www.leatheroticakeywest.com*

10 AIDS Memorial
Squares of black granite are engraved with the names of about a thousand Conchs who have been taken by the disease, along with some poignant, inspirational poetry. 🔊 *Atlantic Ocean end of White Street*

Exclusively gay and lesbian accommodations are available in Key West – See p153

Left **Sloppy Joe's** Right **The Bull**

Top 10 Bars, Pubs, and Clubs

1 Sloppy Joe's
You can get a full meal as well as just a drink at this prominently situated and always noisy bar. It's heavy on Hemingway memorabilia, since he used to hang out here as well as at the original Sloppy Joe's (see below). ⊗ *201 Duval St, Key West • 305-294-5717*

2 Captain Tony's Saloon
This was the original Sloppy Joe's, where Hemingway was a regular. Live bands feature all the time; Conch hero Jimmy Buffett used to sing here. ⊗ *428 Greene St, Key West • 305-294-1838*

3 Green Parrot Bar
Established in 1890 and still going strong. Lots of locals, pool tables, the grotty interior so loved in Key West, and all kinds of live music on weekends. ⊗ *601 Whitehead St., Key West • 305-294-6133*

4 The Bull
Three bars in one, on three different floors. Street level always has some live entertainment going on, while the top floor open deck is the Garden of Eden, the famous clothing-optional bar *(see pp49 & 117)*. ⊗ *224 Duval St, Key West • 305-296-4545*

5 Hog's Breath Saloon
One of the best-known bars due to a far-reaching ad campaign – it's part of a Florida chain. Expect lots of heavy drinking and live music every night. ⊗ *400 Front St, Key West • 305-292-2032*

6 Margaritaville
Local-boy-made-good Jimmy Buffett is the owner of this bar-restaurant-souvenir shop. There's live music nightly, and on occasion the Parrot Head leader himself shows up. ⊗ *500 Duval St, Key West • 305-292-1435*

7 Top Lounge
Located on the seventh floor of the Holiday Inn La Concha Hotel, the Top Lounge is one of the best places to get a 360-degree view of the island and beyond, drink in hand. You can also go up for the view when the bar is closed. ⊗ *430 Duval St, Key West • 305-296-2991*

8 Schooner Wharf Bar
This bar is located in the Historic Seaport District, offering open-air views of the waterfront and live music all the time. ⊗ *202 William St., Key West • 305-292-9520*

9 Rumrunners
The multi-level venue offers live rock, indoor and outdoor dance floors, some good DJs, and decent food at decent prices. ⊗ *201 Duval St, Key West • 305-292-1795*

10 Epoch
Epoch has seven bars on two levels, a state-of-the-art light show, and the biggest dance floor in Florida, featuring hip-hop and techno sounds. There's a Foam Party every Thursday night. ⊗ *623 Duval St, Key West • 305-296-8521*

Dorothy's Deli

Price Categories

For a three course meal for one with half a bottle of wine (or equivalent meal), taxes, and extra charges.

$	under $20
$$	$20–$40
$$$	$40–$55
$$$$	$55–$80
$$$$$	over $80

🔟 Conch Dining

1 The Catch
Sublime fusion cuisine in a romantic setting just off Duval. The basil-braised portabello mushroom with chèvre cheese and balsamic honey glaze is an unforgettable appetizer; try one of the seafood pastas for the main course. ✎ *530 Simonton St, Key West • 305-295-9300 • $$$*

2 Rick's Blue Heaven
You'll never forget the charm and delicious food at this wonderful place *(see p26)*.

3 Mangoes
A meal here is not to be missed, not only for the exciting food – such as their signature wild mushroom and truffle "martini" – but also because the place is so central to Key West life. ✎ *700 Duval St., Key West • 305-292-4606 • $$$*

4 Louie's Backyard
Haute cuisine in a breezy, easy setting right on the Atlantic. Enticing menu items include arugula and spinach with sweet-hot mustard vinaigrette and crispy duck wontons, and knock-out desserts. ✎ *700 Waddell Ave, Key West • 305-294-1062 • $$$*

5 Pier House Restaurant
The chef utilizes the abundance of ingredients indigenous to the Caribbean and the Florida peninsula, but prepares them with a flourish that redefines regional cuisine. The lobster with marinated plantain is a tour de force. ✎ *Pier House Resort, 1 Duval St, Key West • 305-296-4600 • $$$$*

6 El Siboney
Great Cuban food in abundance in a friendly, no-nonsense setting. Lots of diversity, such as roast pork with casava and *tamale*, breaded *palomilla* steak, or stuffed crab. ✎ *900 Catherine St, Key West • 305-296-4184 • $*

7 Duval Beach Club
Owned by actress Kelly McGillis, this restaurant-snack bar is easy-going and pleasant, serving mostly sandwiches, salads, and great breakfasts. ✎ *1405 Duval St, Key West • 305-295-6550 • $$*

8 Awful Arthur's
Great oysters, crab legs, spicy steamed peel-and-eat shrimp, clams, mussels, crawfish, conch fritters, and Island rum drinks to wash it all down. ✎ *On Angela St, right off Duval • 305-293-7663 • $$*

9 Camille's
Homemade buckwheat pancakes or fresh snapper with a nut crust help make this a favorite for Sunday brunch among the Conch cognoscenti. ✎ *11202 Simonton St, Key West • 305-296-4811 • $$*

🔟 Dorothy's Deli
Sandwiches made to order and a selection of homemade salads and sweets, and all the various munchies you need for a great picnic. ✎ *723 Simonton, at Petronia, Key West • 305-292-6944 • $*

Note: *Unless otherwise stated, all restaurants have disabled access, accept credit cards, and serve vegetarian meals*

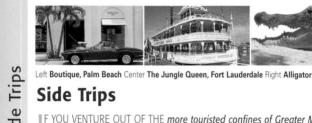

Left **Boutique, Palm Beach** Center **The Jungle Queen, Fort Lauderdale** Right **Alligator**

Side Trips

I
F YOU VENTURE OUT OF THE *more touristed confines of Greater Miami, be
ready for some mild culture shock. Not only is the rough-and-ready Native
American way of life on the Everglades reservations apparent, but even the
Gulf Coast and Treasure Coast enclaves can seem to exist
in a world apart. Gone entirely is the international
feel, and in its place is a sense of the old Florida.*

Via Roma, Palm Beach

View of the Gold Coast

its inception has been called the Tamiami Trail, which sounds like a Native American word but simply stands for Tampa-Miami, the cities connected by the road. However, it does take you deep into Seminole country, where you can experience the wonders of the Everglades. As you make your way to the Gulf coast, be sure to stop at Everglades City and Naples (see p128). ◈ Map A3–C4

1 A1A North along the Gold Coast

Starting just at the northern tip of Miami Beach is a stretch of beautiful, wealthy communities that goes on for at least 50 miles (80 km). As diverse in their own ways as the Greater Miami area, they add immeasurably to the cultural richness of South Florida and make an unsurpassed choice for beaching it, too (see pp24–5).

2 The Everglades, across Alligator Alley (I-75)

This is probably the easiest, fastest route across the Everglades: an Interstate toll-road with two lanes of traffic in each direction. It keeps you at arm's length from the swampy, teeming mass of it all, but there are several great stops along the way, as you pass through Big Cypress National Preserve and just to the north of Fakahatchee Strand State Preserve. ◈ Map B–C3

3 The Everglades, across the Tamiami Trail (Hwy 41)

Highway 41 was the first cut across the Everglades and from

4 Loxahatchee National Wildlife Refuge

This is the only surviving remnant of the northern Everglades, a vast area of mostly sawgrass marsh that is so characteristic of the Everglades environment. The inviting public-use areas provide viewing opportunities for a large variety of wetland flora and fauna, including egrets, alligators, and the endangered snail kite. Activities include nature walks, hiking, canoeing, bird-watching, and bass-fishing. A 5-mile (8-km) canoe trail provides the best way to see and explore the refuge up close. ◈ 10216 Lee Road, Boynton Beach • Map C–D 2–3 • 1-800-683-5873 • Sunrise–sunset daily • Adm

Birdlife, the Everglades

For more on the Everglades See pp28–9

Fountain, Palm Beach

5 A1A North along the Treasure Coast

Palm Beach, on the Gold Coast, is the winter playground and shopping mecca of the rich (see p25). If you continue on A1A north of Palm Beach, the megalopolis gives way to the smaller, quieter towns of the Treasure Coast. These include Vero, the largest; Jupiter, which has no barrier islands; Stuart, with its charming historic district; rural-feeling Fort Pierce; and, at the northern extension of the Treasure Coast, the little fishing village of Sebastian. Vist these if you want to experience South Florida beach life without the hurly-burly of Miami. ◈ Map D1–2

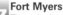

Tiffany Co. clock, Palm Beach

6 Naples and Around

If you cross the Everglades, your inevitable first stop on the Gulf Coast will be Naples. This wealthy beach city prides itself on a manicured beauty, 55 golf courses, and a soigné downtown area. There's a pleasant pier where you can commune with pelicans or do some fishing, and 10 miles (16 km) of pristine, sugary beaches, with warmer waters than the Atlantic. Nearby Marco Island, the most northerly of the Ten Thousand Islands archipelago, is a good base for delving into the western fringe of the Everglades. It has been the source of significant Calusa Native American finds, some dating back 3,500 years. ◈ Map A3

7 Fort Myers

Though the town is historically famous as the base of operations for the 19th-century inventor Thomas Alva Edison, modern Fort Myers has become one of the main escapes for Mid-westerners seeking a holiday by the sea, especially in winter. Its beaches have the feel of Indiana or Iowa about them, full of families without any of the Miami obsessions with style. The only problems you're likely to encounter are traffic snarls. ◈ Map A2

The beach and pier at Naples

Historical mansion, Fort Myers

8 Sanibel and Captiva Islands

The Lee Island Coast offers an irresistible combination of sandy beaches, exotic wildlife, lush vegetation, and wonderful sunsets. The jewels in the crown are Sanibel and Captiva Islands, which offer a Caribbean-style laid-back atmosphere mixed with upscale shops and restaurants. Much of the territory is protected, and development has been limited: there are no condos and very few large hotels, mainly just houses and cottages scattered among the greenery. ⊗ Map A3

9 Dry Tortugas from Key West

You can travel to the wonderful islands of the Dry Tortugas by seaplane or ferry from Key West. Companies offering trips include the Yankee Freedom and the Fast Cat. The day-long tours include food and snorkeling gear. Camping overnight is also possible. The most visited island is Garden Key, the site of Fort Jefferson *(see also p32)*. ⊗ Map A5 • *Yankee Freedom, 305-294-7009 • Fast Cat 1-800-236-7937*

10 Lake Okeechobee

This huge lake – the name means "big water" in the language of the Native American Seminoles – is the second largest

The South Florida Land-Rush

South Florida's warm winter climate and economic upswing of the early 20th century made it seem a perfect place to build the American Dream. The 1920s saw South Florida's first great land boom, when rampant development threatened to make the Everglades a memory. At the height of the boom, prime land could fetch $26,000 per acre, but many would-be investors were bankrupted after being scammed into buying swampland far from the waterfront. The bubble definitely burst with the one-two punch of a hurricane in 1926 and the Great Depression a few years later.

freshwater lake in the US, covering 750 sq miles (1,942 sq km). Though not particularly scenic because of a high dike that was built all the way around it, it is well known for its excellent fishing opportunities. The towns around the lake are relatively undeveloped for tourism, some even rather grim. The best to use as a fishing base is pleasant little Clewiston. The main industry south of the lake is sugar cane – growers are often at odds with environmentalists who are trying to preserve the Everglades. ⊗ Map C2

Fort Jefferson, Dry Tortugas

Alice's at La-Te-Da

⏣ Where to Eat

1 California Café, Fort Lauderdale

California-Mediterranean cooking of a high standard. Innovative dishes include stone crab-stuffed portobello mushrooms. ✪ *Hyatt Regency Pier 66, 2301 SE 17th St Causeway, Fort Lauderdale • Map D3 • 954-728-3500 • $$$*

2 Swamp Water Café, Everglades

Genuine swamp food: alligator tail nuggets, catfish filets, froglegs, and even some local venison. ✪ *Big Cypress Reservation, 20 miles north at exit 14 off I-75 from Ft Lauderdale or Naples • Map B3 • 1-800-949-6101 • $*

3 Rod and Gun Club, Everglades

Set in a classic Florida frontier hotel, with great views. Fresh fish sandwiches (soft-shell crab or succulent grouper) a specialty. ✪ *200 Riverside Dr, Everglades City • Map B4 • 941-695-2101 • No credit cards • No vegetarian options • $$*

4 Café Protegé, West Palm Beach

A gourmet restaurant on the campus of a great culinary school. Try the escargot in a garlic and white wine cream sauce. ✪ *2410 Metrocenter Blvd, West Palm Beach • Map D2 • 561-687-2433 • $$$*

5 Sinclair's Ocean Grill, Jupiter

Indoor or patio dining. The cuisine is traditional Floribbean – a bit of Caribbean, Pacific Rim, and Floridian. ✪ *Jupiter Beach Resort, 5 North A1A, Jupiter • Map D2 • 561-745-7120 • $$$*

6 The Dock at Crayton Cove, Naples

More Floribbean crossover cuisine, with macadamia fried goat cheese and Jamaican jerk chicken quesadilla. ✪ *845 12th Ave S at Naples Bay • Map A3 • 941-263-9940 • $$$*

7 The Veranda, Fort Myers

Charming restaurant, with Deep South décor. The artichoke fritter stuffed with blue crab is outstanding. ✪ *2122 2nd St, Fort Myers • Map A2 • 941-332-2065 • $$$*

8 Key Lime Bistro, Captiva

Fun and funky, with a beachy feel. Dishes include a tri-color vegetarian terrine and chicken voodoo. Sunday jazz brunch, too. ✪ *11509 Andy Rosse Lane, Captiva Island • Map A3 • 941-395-4000 • $$*

9 Alice's at La-Te-Da, Key West

Alice Weingarten creates culinary magic, with her signature fusion cuisine, all set in a romantic garden atmosphere. ✪ *1125 Duval St, Key West • Map A6 • 305-296-6706 • $$$*

10 Colonial Dining Room, Clewiston

Fresh fish from Lake Okeechobee, and a genteel air. Antiques and antebellum-style reproductions abound. ✪ *Clewiston Inn, 108 Royal Palm Ave • Map C2 • 863-983-8151 • $$*

Key West is included here as the access point for the Dry Tortugas – for more Key West restaurants See p125

Price Categories

For a standard double room per night (with breakfast if included), taxes, and extra charges.

$	under $100
$$	$100–$200
$$$	$200–$250
$$$$	$250–$300
$$$$$	over $300

Left **Hyatt Regency** Right **Jupiter Beach Resort**

🔟 Where to Stay

1 Hyatt Regency Pier 66, Fort Lauderdale

Fantastic views from the revolving Pier Top Lounge. Well-appointed rooms, and facilities include a spa and fitness center. ◈ 2301 SE 17th St Causeway, Fort Lauderdale • Map D3 • 1-888-591-1234 • www.hyatt.com • $$$$

2 Billie Swamp Safari Wildlife Park, Everglades

The amenities are little better than camping out, but this is a chance to get up close and personal with the Everglades. ◈ Big Cypress Reservation • Map B3 • 1-800-949-6101 • www.seminoletribe.com • No private baths or air conditioning • $

3 Rod and Gun Lodge, Everglades

Resting quietly in the Everglades, but with a colorful past that includes stays by Hemingway, US presidents, and even Mick Jagger. ◈ 200 Riverside Dr, Everglades City • Map B4 • 941-695-2101 • No credit cards • $$

4 Hibiscus House, West Palm Beach

Victorian décor, exquisite china, and individually outfitted rooms, plus an outstanding pool and patio area. ◈ 501 30th St, West Palm Beach • Map D2 • 1-800-203-4927 • www.hibiscushouse.com • $

5 Jupiter Beach Resort

Plush but unpretentious. The rooms are simple but have marble baths, colorful furnishings, and (mostly) terrific views. Good choice for families. ◈ 5 North A1A, Jupiter • Map D2 • 1-800-228-8810 • www.jupiterbeachresort.com • $$$

6 The Inn on Fifth, Naples

Cozy hotel radiating Mediterranean charm, with lavish fountains and plush interiors. ◈ 699 5th Ave S, Naples • Map A3 • 1-888-403-8778 • www.naplesinn.com • $$$

7 Sanibel Harbour Resort and Spa

Stucco walls, spacious rooms, and a spectacular recreational area, featuring waterfalls and a private beach. ◈ 17260 Harbour Pointe Drive • Map A3 • 1-800-767-7777 • www.sanibel-resort.com • $$$$$

8 Captiva Island Inn

A collection of wood-frame cottages, set among tropical palms and just steps from a faultless beach. ◈ 11509 Andy Rosse Lane, Captiva Island • Map A3 • 1-800-454-9898 • www.captivaislandinn.com • $$

9 Crowne Plaza La Concha, Key West

Tennessee Williams is said to have written *A Streetcar Named Desire* here; presidents and royalty have stayed, too. ◈ 430 Duval St, Key West • Map A6 • 1-800-745-2191 • www.laconchakeywest.com • $$

10 Clewiston Inn

Evokes a pre-Civil War atmosphere with its décor. ◈ 108 Royal Palm Ave • Map C2 • 1-800-749-4466 • www.clewistoninn.com • $

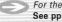

For the main listing of hotels in Miami and the Keys **See pp146–53**

STREETSMART

MIAMI'S TOP 10

Left **Downtown Miami**

🔟 Planning Your Trip

1 When to Go/Climate

With its subtropical climate, South Florida is a year-round destination. However, late spring and summer can be uncomfortably hot, with rain showers almost every afternoon. The high season is from about December to April.

2 Length of Stay

Stay as long as possible. Besides the beach life, South Florida has a great deal to offer, especially in high season, when there seems to be a festival just about every week. Many hotels offer special deals if you stay by the week.

3 What to Bring

If coming from abroad, bring an international driver's license, a voltage converter, and any special prescription medicines you need. Also bring some good walking shoes, or, better yet, sandals. Otherwise, bring as little as possible.

Consulates in Miami

- UK 305-374-1522
- Canada 305-579-1600
- Germany 305-358-0290
- France 305-372-9798
- Italy 305-374-6322
- The Netherlands 305-789-6646
- Spain 305-446-5511
- Israel 305-925-9400
- Japan 305-530-9090

4 Visas and Passports

Members of EU countries have more or less automatic 90-day visas. Other nationals must apply for a nonimmigrant visa from a US consulate. Canadians need only proof of residence. You may need to be able to prove that you have sufficient funds to cover your stay, and, of course, you must have a return ticket.

5 Customs

Allowances for visitors over 21 years of age entering the US are: 1 liter (2 pints) of alcohol, gifts worth up to $100, and 200 cigarettes, 100 cigars (but not Cuban!), or 3 lbs (1.4 kg) of tobacco. A number of goods are prohibited, including cheese, fresh fruit, meat products, and, of course, illegal drugs.

6 Money and Travel Insurance

Travel insurance is essential for foreign visitors – a minimum of $1 million of medical coverage, including accidental death and emergency care, trip cancellation, and baggage or document loss. Travel with as little cash as you can manage, for safety reasons and to avoid questioning by customs officers.

7 Embassies and Consulates

Most major countries have diplomatic offices in Miami. Most consulates are set up to help their nationals if they run into difficulties.

8 Guided Package Tours

Given Miami's dangerous reputation – though considerably improved of late – many travelers prefer to visit as part of an organized group. This can save a great deal of doubt and stress by answering many questions for you in advance. However, be aware that this type of tour tends to put you up in the least appealing parts of town. Choose a group tour that gives you a maximum of flexibility.

9 Weights, Measures, and Time

The US uses the imperial system of ounces, pounds, inches, feet, yards, miles, etc. (This book gives both imperial and metric values.) Voltage is 110-115 volts, and the electrical plugs have two flat prongs. Miami is in the Eastern Time Zone, five hours behind Greenwich Mean Time, and 3 hours ahead of California.

10 Language

Though English is widely spoken in the main tourist areas, bear in mind that the majority of Miamians speak Spanish as their first language. It is worth learning some basic Spanish phrases as a matter of courtesy.

Left **Miami Chamber of Commerce** Center **Key West Chamber of Commerce** Right **Deco Center**

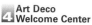 Sources of Information

1 Greater Miami Convention & Visitors' Bureau

The Bureau has both local and international offices, and a website. It offers maps and pointers on everything in the Greater Miami area, including the Keys and the Everglades.

2 General Tips

The Visit Florida and MetroGuide Miami websites are worth a visit.

3 Chambers of Commerce in Miami

Miami Beach, Coral Gables, and Coconut Grove have their own Chambers of Commerce, which offer local maps and information.

4 Art Deco Welcome Center

Guided tours and self-guided tours (including audioguides) are available, as well as literature on the District and Deco style.

5 Tropical Everglades Visitor Association

Tips on tours and walks, fishing and boating, diving and snorkeling, sights and attractions, restaurants and lodgings.

6 Greater Homestead/ Florida City Chamber of Commerce

Provides brochures and discount coupons for the entire South Miami and

Everglades area. The office is housed in a period building with a photo exhibit recounting the history of Homestead. The suggested walk around the historic center is worthwhile.

7 Greater Fort Lauderdale Convention & Visitors Bureau

For information about Fort Lauderdale, Hollywood, Pompano Beach, Sunrise, Lauderdale-By-The-Sea, or Deerfield Beach.

8 Vacation Planner Magazine

The free glossy magazine *Vacation Planner*, covering the South Florida area, is available at many information centers

9 Information About Palm Beach

The Palm Beach Country Convention & Visitors' Bureau has a boatload of materials. Its Chamber of Commerce also publishes an extensive *Official Guide to Palm Beach*.

10 Information About Key West

The Monroe County Tourist Development Council – The Florida Keys & Key West – people know everything about the archipelago, and their love for the area is infectious. They provide the best maps and the top tips for getting the most out of every single mile marker along the way.

Directory

Greater Miami CAVB
701 Brickell Ave, Suite 2700, Miami • 1-800-933-8448 • 0171-978-5233 (UK) • www.tropi cool miami.com

General Tips
www.flausa.com • www. miami.metroguide.net

Chambers of Commerce in Miami
1920 Meridian Ave, Miami Beach, 305-672-1270 • 2333 Ponce de Leon Blvd, Colonade Office Tower, Suite 650, Coral Gables, 305-446-1657 • Peacock Park, nr S Bayshore Drive, Coconut Grove, 305-444-7270

Art Deco Center
*1001 Ocean Drive
• 305-531-3484
• www.mdpl.org*

Everglades (TEVA)
*160 US Hwy 1, Florida City • 1-800-388-9669
• www.tropicalever glades.com*

Greater Homestead
*41-43 North Krome Ave
• 305-242-4814*

Fort Lauderdale
1850 Eller Drive, Suite 303 • 1-800-227-8669

Palm Beach
1555 Palm Beach Lakes Blvd • 561-233-3000

Florida Keys
*1201 White St, Key West • 305-296-1552
• 01564-794999 (UK)
• www.fla-keys.com*

Left **Miami Airport terminal** Center **Shuttle bus** Right **Bridge in the Keys**

🔟 Tips for Arriving in Miami

1 Airlines
Several major international and regional airlines serve the Greater Miami area, among them American, Continental, Delta, United, US Airways, AirTran, and Southwest; and from the UK, British Airways, Northwest, and Virgin Atlantic.

2 Airfares
The airline market in the US is quite volatile, with newcomers entering it every year, so bargains can be found – especially with a little time spent searching the Internet. Currently, for domestic flights, AirTran and Southwest are good. Flying midweek is usually cheaper.

3 Miami International Airport
One of the busiest in the world, which can mean long lines at immigration. There may be lots of walking to do, too. There are tourist information desks and car rental counters outside the customs area, but they are not always staffed when you need them.

4 Fort Lauderdale-Hollywood International Airport
This is the area's second airport, less crowded but just as convenient and served by almost as many airlines as Miami Airport. It's the perfect choice if you're staying along the southern part of the Gold Coast.

5 Car Rental, Taxis, and Shuttle Buses
Options for getting from the airports into Miami are numerous: rental cars, shuttle services *(see below)*, taxis, limousines, and shuttle buses to the Metrorail and TriRail lines.

6 SuperShuttle
This company, and other competitors, offers 24-hour door-to-door service for much less than the cost of a taxi. The catch is that you have to share with other travelers, so you may have to ride around for a bit while others are picked up or dropped off. You can book your pick-up on their website.

7 By Car
The major Interstates that lead to Miami are I-95, down the north coast, and I-75, from the Gulf coast. There's also Florida's Turnpike, which shoots down from Central Florida. These highways are well maintained, with welcome centers along the way. Highways 1, A1A, and 41 are not efficient choices unless you're exploring the Greater Miami area.

8 By Sea
The Port of Miami is, quite simply, the largest in the world. From here endless mammoth cruise ships depart for romantic Caribbean adventures. People arriving by private yacht have a choice of excellent marinas.

9 By Train
Amtrak serves Miami from everywhere in the US. Sleepers and restaurant service are available. For train service within the Miami area, there's the excellent Tri-Rail, which hooks up with the Metrorail system up and down the Gold Coast.

10 By Bus
There's a bus station near the airport and one Downtown, at 100 NW 6th St, served by Greyhound, Trailways, and Metrobus. The buses are cheap but not very convenient if you have much luggage. Greyhound is a decent, though fairly slow, option for getting from Miami to Key West.

Directory

Miami International Airport
305-876-7000

Fort Lauderdale/ Hollywood Airport
954-359-1200

Palm Beach Airport
561-471-7412

SuperShuttle
1-800-258-3826 or 305-871-2000 • www.super shuttle.com

Tri-Rail
1-800-273-7545

Amtrak Railroad
1-800-872-7245

Greyhound and Trailways Bus
1-800-231-2222 for both

Left **Metromover** Center **Cyclists** Right **Vehicles to rent**

🔟 Tips for Getting Around Miami

1 Metrobus System
The Metrobus routes cover the whole Miami-Dade area, but don't expect them to hold to any schedule, or to come even once every hour. You'll need the correct change, a token, or a Metropass.

2 Metrorail and Metromover
Metrorail is a 21-mile (34-km) elevated rail system running from Hialeah in the north to Dadeland in the south. It serves Downtown, Coconut Grove, and Coral Gables. Metromover is a monorail extension of Metrorail that runs a circuit around Downtown (see p86).

3 Electrowave
This electric shuttle service is a fast, scenic way to get around South Beach. There are two separate routes, via Collins and Washington avenues. The cars are air-conditioned and smooth.

4 Taxis and Water Taxis
Taxi meters start at $1.50 and click away speedily at $2 a mile, so they're not a good deal for long distances. In Fort Lauderdale you may well decide to try a water taxi, just for the fun of exploring the "Venice of America."

5 Skate, Bicycle, and Scooter Rental
These zippy modes of transportation are definitely the top choices for "doing" South Beach. Many stores will suggest self-guided tours and offer free skating lessons. If you want to ride the American Dream, rent a motorbike.

6 Rental Cars
Car rental in Florida can be expensive, but you can get better deals by looking for fly-drive packages, or by booking through the Internet in advance of your arrival. You'll need a valid driver's license, photo ID, and a credit card (cash or a debit card are rarely accepted). Watch out for hidden extras.

7 Road Rules
Freeways and toll-roads in Miami are generally good and fairly easy to negotiate, but the local drivers are another thing. Lane-changing at top speeds is a local sport, as are all sorts of other erratic habits. The result can be myriad fender-benders and some terrible traffic snarls.

8 City Tours
Double-decker tour buses hug the coast from Aventura Mall in the north down to Coconut Grove, with stops at every significant point.

9 Limousines
Being a star-studded place, stretch limos are a common sight here, the longer the better.

10 Navigation
The grid system of road orientation and numbers (NW, SE, 1st, 2nd, Ave, St, etc) begins Downtown, with Flagler Street as one axis and Miami Avenue as the other. Confusingly, Miami Beach has its own system, as does Coral Gables, and many streets have one or even two extra names.

Directory

Miami-Dade Metro Transit
305-770-3131

Metrobus System
305-770-3131

Electrowave
305-535-9160

Miami Taxis
305-444-4444, 305-888-8888, or 305-888-7777

Fort Lauderdale Water Taxi
954-467-6677

Bike and Roll
760 Washington St
• 305-538-2121

Harley Rentals
1-888-736-8433

Miami Tourist Bus
81 NE 21st Street
• 305-573-8687

Limousines
• Red Carpet Transportation, 305-444-4635
• Carey Limousine Service, 305-893-9850
• Limousines of South Florida, 305-940-5252

Left **The Miami Herald** Center **Mallory Square event, Key West** Right **Drop bins, Palm Beach**

Media Sources

1 The Miami Herald
This daily newspaper is Florida's largest, and its weekly supplements *The Street* and *Weekend* are major sources of information about local entertainment and events.

2 Miami New Times
This is the main free alternative weekly, which you can pick up in many restaurants, stores, clubs, and drop bins all over town. It reviews restaurants, movies, clubs, etc.

3 Key West
The island's eponymous weekly newspaper features news about upcoming events, arts, theater, attractions, music, clubs, local news, features, and opinions. And like all true Conch undertakings, it's notoriously iconoclastic, taking on the local police and other authorities in articles.

4 El Nuevo Herald
This is Miami's Spanish-language edition, which naturally focuses more on issues and events relating to the huge Hispanic community.

5 Hotel Magazines
In the "tonier" hotels, you'll often find *Ocean Drive* and *Where*. The former is not much more than a super-stylish fashion vehicle. *Where* is an international publication – the Miami version, which comes out monthly, has some excellent basic insights and even some captivating articles. Note, however, that all the restaurant listings are there because the owners paid to be included, rendering the reviews less than entirely genuine.

6 Network TV
The programming of the main national networks are carried by four Miami channels: Channel 4 is CBS, Channel 6 is NBC, Channel 7 is FOX, and Channel 10 is ABC. Unless your TV is connected to cable, this will be the configuration for receiving all the regularly scheduled sitcoms, sports, and news programming. The PBS station is normally Channel 2.

7 Cable TV
Most TVs you encounter in Miami will be connected to one cable company or another. Most likely this will mean that you receive not only the major networks but also CNN and MSNBC for news, ESPN for sports, the Weather Channel, Comedy Central, and Nickelodeon (for the kids). You might also be lucky enough to get all or some of the innovative HBO programming, as well as excellent Showtime offerings.

8 English FM Radio
Miami may seem mostly Spanish-speaking, but when you turn on the radio, you'll find that most of the banter is still in English. There's the usual big-city mix of country, oldies, new rock, hard rock, jazz, and NPR (National Public Radio) programming and similar local stations, for people who want to hear the topics of the day intelligently considered by interesting thinkers.

9 Spanish FM Radio
There are, of course, several Spanish-language stations, featuring very high-energy programming and the compelling, nonstop rhythms of every sort of Latin American music, from more or less traditional to the very latest international Latino heartthrobs. It's not a bad way to practice your Spanish, particularly because some of the time the announcers are speaking an easy mixture of Spanish and English, often called Spanglish.

10 AM Radio
Since the quality of the FM signal is so much better – and allows for true stereophonic broadcasting – the AM dial in Miami is given over almost entirely to talk radio. Listeners call in to let off steam about whatever topic of the day the commentator has selected to get everyone worked up about. There are both English and Spanish talk radio stations in Miami.

Left **Emergency Room sign** Center **Shades in the sun** Right **Lifeguard**

Ways to Stay Healthy and Safe

1 Emergency Numbers

The emergency number 911 is toll free, including from payphones.

2 Security Measures

Always keep your antennae out for potential trouble *(see p140)*. Park in well-lit areas, and keep doors locked and windows closed while driving. Make sure you know where you're going, or at least give that impression. Don't go into uncertain neighborhoods at night.

3 Mugging

If you follow the basic precautions, you're unlikely even to come close to being mugged violently, but do watch out for less aggressive crime. Pickpockets work the crowds, so keep valuables tucked away.

4 Walk-in Medical Services

Most area hospitals operate 24-hour emergency rooms, and there are a number of walk-in clinics. Look in the *Yellow Pages* under "Clinics." You can find 24-hour pharmacies in most areas.

5 Sunburn

The sun is intense here, especially when near the reflective beach and water. Wear sunblock or at least sunscreen at all times, and a hat. Avoid heatstroke by drinking plenty of liquids and knowing when it's time to head for shade.

6 Insects

Biting and stinging insects, including annoying mosquitoes, can be a real nuisance between June and November. Wear insect repellent, especially when striking out for the Everglades. Other nasty critters are sand flies, which bite in the evening, and fire ants.

7 Riptides and Undertows

Some areas along the Atlantic have rough surf or are subject to strong currents. Small children, in particular, might be better off in some of the more protected waters away from the ocean, especially the gentle Keys waters.

8 Jellyfish, Stingrays, and Sharks

Stinging jellyfish, in particular the man-o-war, sometimes frequent the waters off the coast. Be careful of the ones washed up on the shore, too. Shark attacks are thankfully quite rare. Stingrays are generally gentle creatures, but be careful not to accidentally tread on one.

9 Hurricanes

Hurricanes are infrequent but devastating. If one should occur, follow the announcements on TV and radio, or call the National Hurricane Center.

10 Lost Property

Even though you have only a slim chance of retrieving lost property, report all lost or stolen items to the police. Keep a copy of the police report to claim insurance later. Most credit card companies have toll-free numbers for reporting a loss, as do traveler's check companies *(see p141)*. If you lose a passport, contact your embassy or consulate *(see p134)*.

Directory

Any Emergency
911

Dentist Referrals
305-667-3647

Clinics
Miami Beach Medical Clinic, 1540 Washington Ave, 305-532-4122
• Today's Woman Medical Center, 3250 S Dixie Hwy, Coconut Grove, 305-441-0304

Hospitals:
South Shore Hospital, 630 Alton, South Beach, 305-672-2100
• Mercy Hospital, 3663 S Miami Ave, Coconut Grove, 305-854-4400
• Coral Gables Hospital, 3100 Douglas Rd, 305-445-8461

National Hurricane Center
305-229-4470

Miami Airport Lost and Found
305-876-7377

For special hotlines and helplines See p144

Left **Respite from the scorching sun** Center **Remember to tip the concierge** Right **Law enforcer**

Things to Avoid

1 Bad Neighborhoods
Most of these areas are in the northern part of Greater Miami, but be aware that just two to three blocks from popular Coco Village, the so-called "Black Grove" is unfortunately quite rundown and dangerous.

2 Bigotry
In outlying areas, outside the bubbles of Miami Beach, Greater Miami and Key West sophistication, you suddenly find yourself in Old Florida, where values can still be quite prejudicial if you are in any way "alternative."

3 Age Restrictions
Ordering alcoholic beverages in a bar if you are under 21, and having alcohol on the beach at any age are strictly prohibited. Needless to say, drunk driving is also entirely unacceptable – often roadblocks are set up on causeways leaving Miami Beach to nab suspicious drivers.

4 Smoking
Buying tobacco if you are under 18 is against the law in Florida. Not that it makes much difference if you're a smoker because smoking in public buildings is illegal, and they're also considering making it illegal to smoke in restaurants and bars. Many hotels are entirely non-smoking.

5 Forgetting to Tip
Tipping is not an option in the US. Waiters and waitresses get minimum wage or less in the US and depend on whatever tips they clear. Very rarely, the gratuity will be automatically added to your bill, so check. If not, 15 percent of the total before taxes for lunch, and 20 percent for dinner is considered about right.

6 Looking Like a Tourist
To avoid the dangers of pick-pocketing, as well as the nuisance of being accosted by the occasional panhandler, try not to appear to be lost, and don't load yourself down with too much stuff, such as bags, cameras, maps, etc. How you dress is really not such an issue here, as everyone tends to dress down – lots of men even go shirtless all over South Beach streets. One thing that's a definite fashion no-no, however, is wearing socks with your sandals.

7 Forgetting Your Sunscreen
If you didn't bring any sunscreen or sunblock with you, go out immediately and buy a good one. Sunburn is the number one health hazard here, and the sun will get you, you are not an exception. Be sure to apply sunscreen liberally and often, especially to the exposed areas you tend to overlook. If you go to the nude beaches, that advice goes double!

8 The Velvet Rope
Standing in line at a popular club can be a real drag – and you might not get in at all. Talk to your hotel concierge about getting you into the VIP lounge of the club of your choice. For a little extra money, you can save yourself a lot of time and potential disappointment.

9 Law Enforcement
Getting on the wrong side of the Miami cops is never a good idea. There are three separate law enforcement agencies here – city police, county sheriffs, and the highway patrol, and they are generally friendly and helpful, in the spirit of promoting Miami's image as a tourist mecca. However, in the same spirit, if they suspect you are a trouble-maker, they can be notoriously harsh.

10 AIDS
Sex without a condom in this pleasure-loving area is a really bad idea. Miami has the highest incidence of AIDS in the US, according to a 2002 study. Fortunately, most of the bars, especially the gay ones, have big bowls full of free condoms for patrons to help themselves to.

Left **ATM** Center **Sign for mail** Right **Phonecard**

🔟 Money and Communication Tips

1 Exchanging Money

Except for American Express, there are virtually no exchange places as such, but you can go into any bank to exchange money. All in all, however, it's best to avoid this ritual (see below).

2 Automated Teller Machines

This is the most sensible way to get the cash you need. If you have an ATM card of any sort, chances are it will work in almost any machine and you will be able to draw cash out any time, up to your daily limit. There will be a fee, but the time and hassle you save is worth it. Don't forget your PIN!

3 Credit Cards

Doing anything in the US without a credit card is almost unthinkable, especially in a hotel.

4 Travelers' Checks

As a backup, travelers' checks can be useful, but these days they are outdated and almost pointless.

5 Banks

Banks are numerous and all have walk-up ATM machines handily located. If you must perform some sort of transaction inside, the hours are usually 9am–4pm, Monday to Friday, and sometimes later on Thursdays. Some banks are also open on Saturday mornings.

6 Sales Tax

Unlike in some countries, sales tax is not included in the marked price of anything, including restaurant meals. The only items sales tax is not added to are most groceries. Florida's sales tax at present is 6 percent, but local taxes can bump that up considerably. Hoteliers in Miami add on 12.5 percent to your bill.

7 Public Phones

You'll find these at gas stations, restaurants, hotels, on the sidewalk, and elsewhere. For long distance calls, it's easier to use a phonecard, which you can buy from any convenience store. Using your credit card is possible, too, but pricey. For making any call in Miami, even next door, you must dial the 305 area code, but not the 1 before it.

8 Cell Phones

If your cell phone (mobile) is not compatible with US networks, then renting a cell phone to use while here is a sensible option. You'll find vendors at the airport upon arrival.

9 Postal Services

Post offices are usually open from 9am–5pm on weekdays, with some open on Saturday mornings, too. Stamps are sold in many drugstores, hotels, and department stores. All domestic mail goes first class, and you should use airmail for any overseas mail. If you want it to get there the next day in the US, go for Express Mail.

10 Fax and Internet Access

Internet cafés abound. Many hotels, and especially hostels, offer the service, too, usually for a charge. A good central Internet point in South Beach, just a block from the sand, is South Beach Internet. It's also a lounge and a decent restaurant where a certain amount of people-watching goes on – after all, it's SoBe!

Directory

American Express
330 Biscayne Blvd., Downtown • 305-358-7350 • 9–5:30 Mon–Fri, 9–5 Sat

Lost Credit Cards
VISA 1-800-336-8472 • MasterCard 1-800-843-0777 • American Express 1-800-528-4800 • Discover 1-800-347-2683 • Diners Club, 1-800-234-6377

Lost Travelers' Checks
American Express 1-800-221-7282 • Thomas Cook 1-800-223-7373.

SoBe Internet Café
1100 Collins Ave • 305-532-4331

Unusually, the Miami 305 phone code must be dialled even when in the city, so remember to use it when making calls.

Left **Center for tourist information** Center **Cheap eats** Right **Bicycling**

Ways to Save Money

1 Fly-Drive Packages

To get the most out of Miami, you need a car. Some of the fly-drive packages can save a great deal of money.

2 Off-Season

There's no doubt that visiting the area out of season costs much, much less. Hotel prices can be reduced by up to two-thirds. It's true that the weather is a lot muggier, but the ocean breezes make beach life tolerable, and everything else is air-conditioned. Also ask your travel agent or check the web for promotional fares, but be sure to get all the details.

3 Discount Booklets

Coupon brochures – often with useful maps – are available free at most tourist stops or information desks. Savings can often be significant if you've got a large group or family to pay for. There are sometimes accommodations and tour discount coupons, too.

4 Free Sights

Not much is free here, apart from the stupendous beaches. But there are parks and gardens that charge no admission, and strolling around the busy streets doesn't have to involve any outlay. One of the greatest pleasures is watching the ships go by, either from the bottom of Miami Beach, at South Pointe, or from Mallory Square in Key West.

5 Saving Money on Accommodations

It's always worth trying to bargain the price down a bit, since no rates are cast in concrete. You can get an especially good deal in many places if you negotiate a weekly rate. If you're traveling on business of any kind, you can also request a commercial rate.

6 Cheap Eats

Although there are many very expensive restaurants in South Florida, there are many more chain fast-food franchises. If such fare disagrees with your palate, you'll also find excellent local eateries that charge relatively little for good sandwiches and such. Otherwise, think of picnics and pick up supplies at the local market or grocery.

7 Picnicking

You can have your picnic anywhere that there isn't a sign forbidding it. Many public parks and all state parks have tables and other facilities, often really pleasant ones, and you can take your snack to the beach with you, too. However, be aware that littering in the US is severely frowned upon, so dispose of all refuse in the bins provided.

8 Pay in Cash

Often when making a purchase of any kind, especially in a shop, you can negotiate a discount if you pay in cash, rather than by credit card. The shopkeeper will be saving the charge from the credit card company and willing to pass on some of that saving – usually 2–5 percent – to you.

9 Bicycling

Not only is it healthier, allowing you to work on your tan and breathe in the energy-charged air here, but it's also one of the very best ways to get around most of the prime areas in South Florida. Biking around South Beach, Key Biscayne, Key West, and even along certain trails in the Everglades is, for many, the only way to go, and the money you can save is significant.

10 Shop Wisely

Whatever you're in the market for, from tickets to trinkets, take the time to do a little research and price-comparison. Chances are you can find the same or similar item for much less if you shop around. If it's a toiletry need, for example, head for one of the large, all-purpose drugstores, where there are generic brands of almost everything, from contact lens solution to mouthwash, usually at half the name-brand price.

Left **Disabled sign** Right **"Kneeling" bus**

🔟 Senior and Disabled Travelers

1 Retirees
For decades, all of Florida has been retirement heaven – or "God's Waiting-Room," as it's sometimes not so graciously called. Hence, there are many facilities for senior citizens.

2 Senior Travelers
Traveling in South Florida is relatively easy for seniors, and there are good programs to allow seniors to get the most out of their experience here. Contact Elderhostel and Interhostel.

3 Tips for Seniors
Take advantage of the extra time you've earned, allowing yourself to get to know Miami in greater depth than the fly-by tourist. Use the cooler modes of getting around – on South Beach the air-conditioned Electrowave, and on Key West the shaded and breezy Conch Tour Train.

4 Resources for Seniors
Membership in the American Association of Retired Persons is open to US and Canadian residents age 50 or over. They provide up-dated travel information and discounts. Elderhostel and Interhostel are for people 60 and over.

5 Discounts and Freebies
Senior citizens are eligible for discounts on travel, car rental, accommodations, museum entrance, and more. Take your ID. Sometimes the definition of "senior" can be as young as 55! If you're a US citizen or permanent resident, get a Golden Age Passport, which entitles you to free entry into all national parks, monuments, and historic sites.

6 Disabled Travelers
Generally speaking, the area is well-set-up for disabled travelers. Mobility International USA and the Society for the Advancement of Travelers with Handicaps (SATH) have more information.

7 Accessibility to Buildings
All public buildings in the US are required by law to provide wheelchair access. However, older Deco hotels and many of the old guesthouses might have only one disabled-accessible room.

8 Transportation
Public buses "kneel," and the other public forms of transportation also have wheelchair access. Some taxis and car rental companies have special equipment: ask in advance.

9 Tips for the Disabled
For getting around such areas as South Beach or Key West, take full advantage of electrically powered transport, either your own wheelchair or a rented one. The heat and humidity can make exertion uncomfortable.

10 Resources for the Disabled
Check out Access-Able, Directions Unlimited, and Wheels Up! on the Internet. Also call Miami-Dade Disability Services, Deaf Services Bureau, and the Miami Lighthouse for the Blind.

Directory

Miami-Dade Elder Help Line
305-670-4357

The American Association of Retired Persons
1-800-424-3410

Elderhostel
1-877-426-8056

Interhostel
1-800-733-9753

Mobility Websites
• www.miusa.org
• www.sath.org
• www.access-able.com
• www.wheelsup.com

Miami-Dade Disability Services and Independent Living
305-547-5444

Deaf Services Bureau
305-668-4407

Miami Lighthouse for the Blind
305-856-2288

The Access Hotline
305-358-4357

Left **Local cops** Center **Turtle – look out for injured wildlife** Right **Gay nightclubbers**

TOP 10 Hotlines and Helplines

Directory

Switchboard of Miami
305-358-4357

Team Metro Citizen
305-375-5656

Miami Time & Weather
305-324-8811

Fish & Wildlife Commission
1-800-432-2046

Poison Control
1-800-282-3171

Gay Anti-Violence Hotline
305-358-4357.

First Call for Help/Crisis Line
305-358-4357

The Teen Link Line
305-377-8336, for tapes, 305-377-8255 to speak to a counselor

Parent HelpLine
1-800-345-5044

Florida Child Care
1-888-540-5437

Runaway Hotline (Miami Bridge)
305-635-8953

Teach More, Love More (24 hours)
305-631-8111

Rape Hotline
305-585-7273

Rape Treatment Center:
305-585-5185

Miami-Dade Central Intake and Detoxification
305-638-6540

1 General Medical and Police

The all-purpose number for any emergency is 911. For less acute situations, use the hotlines and helplines listed here.

8 General Helplines

The 24-hour Switchboard of Miami and Team Metro Citizen have information about local services.

9 Miami Time and Weather

If you're planning an outdoor activity of any sort, you can look in the newspaper or online to see the weather forecast. The best way to get the most current report on weather conditions and probabilities is to the call the special number for the Greater Miami area.

10 Injured Wildlife

In your outdoor exploration of South Florida, particularly on the beaches, waterways, or in the Everglades, you may encounter injured animals or birds, large or small. You can call the Fish and Wildlife Commission to get help for them.

2 Poison Helpline

The poison control helpline gives quick advice on antidotes and how to handle any crisis related to poisoning, including food poisoning and allergic reactions.

3 Gay Anti-Violence

The Gay Anti-Violence Hotline offers support and referral services to gay and bisexual victims of harassment, domestic violence, sexual assault, and hate crimes that occur anywhere in the Greater Miami Area.

4 Psychological Crisis Line

Miami provides a First Call for Help/Crisis Line, which is like a 911 line for psychological or emotional problems and dilemmas.

5 Help for Parents and Children

The Teen Link Line aims to provide "Straight Up Information on Stuff that Matters" to teens, with 80 taped informational messages on topics of concern to adolescents and links to counselors. There are also the toll-free Parent HelpLine, the Florida Child Care line, Runaway Hotline, and Teach More, Love More line.

6 Rape Crisis Lines

Counseling is provided for any sort of trauma relating to sexuality and sexual abuse.

7 Drug and Alcohol Counseling

The Miami-Dade Central Intake and Detoxification Center is geared up to take calls from anyone suffering from substance abuse problems.

Left **Hotel lobby** Center **Motel** Right **Parking lot**

Accommodation Tips

1 Area Options

Every sort of accommodation is available in South Florida, from a simple dorm bed in a hostel to a villa in an unbelievably luxurious resort on its own island. Most of the hotels, motels, and the like are on or near the beach, or at least some body of water. Inland, good choices might put you in an interesting and colorfully ethnic urban area, or in a quaint old Everglades town.

2 Needs and Desires

The best way to decide what suits you best is to read up on this fascinatingly rich destination. If it's the outdoors and sports you're after, head directly for the Keys. If it's world-class nightlife, the choice is South Beach.

3 Price Range

The price range is vast. Even on South Beach in high season, just two blocks from the beach, you can find a room for two, with private bath, for as little as $25 per person per night. Or, a block away, a penthouse suite in some fabulous Deco landmark is up for $2,500.

4 Special Deals

Be aware that many hotels have a minimum stay requirement, but often offer a good deal if you book by the week.

5 Making Reservations

If you want to go for the bargain accommodations in high season, it's crucial that you book as early as you possibly can. Make sure the reservation is solid by guaranteeing it with a credit card, and doubly confirming it by way of both fax and email. If you're expecting to arrive late, find out the latest acceptable arrival time before your reservation is subject to cancellation.

6 Without Reservations

Trying to find something on the spot from December to April is not recommended, at least not in South Beach or Key West, especially on weekends. It might take a long time to find, and you run the risk of having to pay even more than top dollar. Taking pot luck is only a good idea in low season.

7 Tipping

The usual practice is to tip the bellboy $1 per bag, both when he brings your luggage to your room and when you depart. If you leave your luggage in storage, the tip should be the same. If your hotel has valet parking, you should tip the guy $2 or so each time he delivers your car to you. If you enjoyed their service, you can also tip the front desk staff and concierge whatever feels right.

8 Hidden Extras

There can be many of these, so get it all clear from the start. If there's valet parking, that can cost about $15–20 per day. Phone calls made from your room phone generally start at 50 cents each, and can be charged on a per-minute basis in some cases. Finally, when you check out, you will notice a rather hefty hotel tax of at least 10 percent has been added on, depending on where the hotel is in South Florida.

9 Traveling with Kids

Family travel is the bread-and-butter of South Florida tourism, and every major hotel or resort offers a wide range of activities and services – supervised play areas, baby-sitting, special games, coloring books, etc. Usually children under a certain age (sometimes as high as 18) can stay free in their parents' room. In addition, many restaurants offer kids' meals at reduced prices.

10 Parking

Valet parking is convenient, but often terribly expensive, and it's impossible to keep the 24-hour meters fed. The only sensible option is to put your car in a parking garage, where you can get a more reasonable rate, and leave it.

Left **Biltmore Hotel** Center **The Breakers** Right **Wyndham Grand Bay Hotel**

Hotels: The Lap of Luxury

1 Loews
SoBe's biggest Deco tower, newly built, is located on a sandy beach in the heart of it all. The multifaceted property incorporates an old hotel – the rebuilt St. Moritz – six restaurants and an outlandishly beautiful, mosaic-tile, oceanfront swimming pool. ◎ *1601 Collins Ave, South Beach • 1-800-235-6397 • www. loewshotels.com • $$$$$*

2 The Shore Club
Very coolly chic, almost Zen-like ambience to this distinctive 1949 Deco-style hotel. There's a gated pool and private beach access. Rooms are in muted tones and have a serene minimalist feel. Wonderful rooftop spa. ◎ *1901 Collins Ave, South Beach • 1-877-640-9500 • www.shoreclub.com• $$$$*

3 Sheraton Bal Harbour Resort
It's a 10-acre (4-ha) tropical garden with a "mystic" rope bridge suspended over a lagoon and close proximity to Bal Harbour. These and other features have drawn the likes of the Clintons and Bill Gates to choose this high-end paradise when they are in Miami. ◎ *9701 Collins Ave, Bal Harbour • 1-800-999-9898 • www.star woods.com • $$$$$*

4 Hotel Intercontinental Miami
In the heart of the business district, this is

Downtown's finest, with spectacular views and gourmet dining. A huge Henry Moore sculpture adorns the impressive lobby; the comfortable, quiet rooms sport marble bathrooms. ◎ *100 Chopin Plaza, at Biscayne Blvd • 1-800-327-3005 • www. interconti.com • $$$*

5 Biltmore Hotel
A beautiful landmark structure (see p18) with the splendor and glamour of a by-gone era and epicurean pleasures, too, in the Palme d'Or restaurant. Rooms are in the grand European tradition, and you can swim in the world's largest hotel pool. ◎ *1200 Anastasia, Coral Gables • 800-727-1926 • $$$$$*

6 Wyndham Grand Bay Hotel
Of stepped construction like some Aztec temple, and loaded with luxuries, such as Persian carpets, Chinese porcelains, crystal chandeliers, designer furniture, and original art. Luciano Pavarotti has a suite here. ◎ *2669 Bayshore Dr, Coconut Grove • 1-800-996-3426 • www. wyndham.com • $$$$*

7 Mayfair House
Set on top of an exclusive shopping mall, the hotel's large suites have rich mahogany furniture, marble baths, and balconies. The style is a pleasing mix of Spain and the Far East, enhanced

by Art Nouveau touches. ◎ *3000 Florida Ave, Coconut Grove • 1-800-433-4555 • www.mayfairhousehotel. com • $$$$*

8 Four Seasons (Palm Beach)
Possibly the finest service you'll ever experience, from fresh fruit and orchids in your extremely large room with sea view, to a towncar shuttle to and from downtown Palm Beach, and one of the finest restaurants in South Florida. ◎ *Lake Worth • 1-800-432-2335 • www.four seasons.com • $$$$$*

9 The Breakers (Palm Beach)
A Palm Beach landmark of the Gilded-Age tradition, whose décor beautifully evokes the Spanish Revival taste that Flagler brought to Florida in the 1890s. Modern comforts are epitomized by the spa annex. ◎ *1 South County Rd • 888-273-2537 • www. thebreakers.com • $$$$$*

10 Pier House & Caribbean Spa (Key West)
In the heart of the historic Seaport District, the hotel is surrounded by lush tropical gardens. It has four unique bars, three award-winning restaurants, and luxurious Island-colonial style rooms, all with ocean, pool, or garden views. ◎ *One Duval Street, Key West • 1-800-327-8340 • www.pier house. com • $$$$*

On pp146–53 are hotel listings for Miami, Fort Lauderdale, Palm Beach, and the Keys. For more hotels outside Miami See p131

Price Categories

For a standard, double room per night (with breakfast if included), taxes, and extra charges.	
$	under $100
$$	$100–$200
$$$	$200–$250
$$$$	$250–$300
$$$$$	over $300

Left **Delano** Right **Raleigh**

🔟 SoBe Deco-Dence

1 Tides
This fully restored Art Deco landmark hotel, with its distinctive coral rock entrance, is in the heart of all SoBe attractions. The décor is epitomized by cool, white linen and overstuffed sofas and easy chairs in all rooms. Superb service. ✆ 1220 Ocean Drive • 1-800-688-7678 • $$$$$

2 Delano
A very trippy and ultra-luxurious Post-Modern wonder. The original, rather austere white exterior has been restored without any fuss. But inside, the divine madness of Philippe Starke, along with hilarious Dali- and Gaudi-inspired designs have been given room to play. The very chi-chi and daring Blue Door restaurant is co-owned by Madonna. ✆ 1685 Collins Ave • 1-800-555-5001 • www.ianschra gerhotels.com • $$$$$

3 Raleigh
On the pricey side, to be sure, but nothing less than fabulous. The décor has endless style and panache, often with period pieces. The eye-popping swimming pool is immortalized in several Esther Williams movies. ✆ 1775 Collins Ave • 1-800-848-1775 • www.raleigh hotel.com • $$$$$

4 The Hotel
"Tiffany," as proclaimed by the neon tower, was The Hotel's name until the famous jewelry company used. It's so long on style and comfort, designed by Todd Oldham, that it qualifies as a work of art in itself. ✆ 801 Collins Ave • 1-877-843-4683 • www.the hotelofsouthbeach.com • $$$$

5 Nash
One of the more sober Deco edifices, built in 1938 and impeccably restored with every comfort. The rooms are done in a tastefully subdued Post-Modern style by noted designer Peter Pago, who also restored other South Beach landmarks. ✆ 1120 Collins Ave • 305-674-7800 • www. hotelnash.com • $$$

6 Avalon-Majestic
Actually two hotels on opposite corners of 7th Street, these perfectly located Deco bon-bons are excellent value. You're in the middle of SoBe's most popular stretch, and you get comfortable rooms and a complimentary continental breakfast. ✆ 700 Ocean Drive • 1-800-933-3306 • www.southbeach hotels.com • $$

7 Albion
Excellent value, considering the extreme chic that exudes from the cutting-edge restoration of this great Deco original. Check out the pool's peek-a-boo portholes. ✆ 1650 James Ave at Lincoln Rd • 1-877-782-3557 • www.rubellhotels. com • $$

8 Abbey
One of the most appealing of the Deco treasures. The décor is simple and comfortable, and rooms are quiet due to its location off the beaten path. Pluses include a remarkable restaurant and a fitness room. ✆ 300 21st St • 1-888-612-2239 • www. abbeyhotel.com • $$

9 Best Western South Beach
You can't say much for the name, but the property is actually four '30s Art Deco sugar cubes (the Kenmore, Taft, Bel Aire, and Davis) spread over the entire block between 10th and 11th Streets. All are freshly restored and set amid spacious gardens. ✆ 1050 Washington Ave • 1-888-343-1930 • www.best western.com • $$

🔟 The Governor
This Art Deco gem, designed by Henry Hohauser, is excellent value, and located on a quiet side street at the north end of South Beach, next to the Bass Museum and the Miami City Ballet. The rooms are comfortable and unpretentious. ✆ 435 21st St • 1-800-542-0444 • www.island outpost.com • $

For more on SoBe's Art Deco landmarks See pp10–13

Left **Lobby of Eden Roc Renaissance Resort** Right **Boca Raton Resort**

Resorts and Spas

1 The Fisher Island Club

The billionaires who favor this very private island getaway love the extreme exclusivity that its remoteness provides. Personal golf-carts, quiet as a whisper, let you toodle around the many beaches, restaurants, clubs, etc. ✆ *Fisher Island Dr (off the MacArthur Causeway – free car ferry every 15 mins)* • *1-800-537-3708* • *$$$$$*

2 Fontainebleau Hilton Resort & Towers, Miami Beach

One of the great Miami Beach hotels, built in the '50s. The restoration is now complete, and the effect is stunning. Rooms are large, and there's a huge beachside spa. ✆ *4833 Collins Ave* • *1-800-548-8886* • *www.hilton.com* • *$$$$*

3 Eden Roc Renaissance Resort and Spa, Miami Beach

In Nautical-Deco style, this is one of Miami Beach's "Queen Mums." It's been entirely renovated and the eternal elegance shines through. This is where Frank Sinatra, Dean Martin, Sammy Davis, Jr., and their chums used to stay. ✆ *4525 Collins Ave., Miami Beach* • *1-800-327-8337* • *www.renaissance hotels.com* • *$$$$*

4 Sonesta Resort, Key Biscayne

Like a giant Mayan temple facing on the Atlantic, this sparkling white highrise is just what families are looking for: a perfect private beach, Olympic-size pool, *chikee* (Native-American) "village," whirlpool baths, and a host of programs for kids and adults. ✆ *350 Ocean Dr, Key Biscayne* • *1-800-766-3782* • *www.sonesta. com* • *$$$$$*

5 Turnberry Isle, Aventura

Very grand, indeed, with oriental carpets, marble accents, and hundreds of acres of landscaped islands and waterways, a golf course, tennis courts, spa, private beach, and harbor. The feeling is clubby, welcoming, and very, very rich. ✆ *19999 W Country Club Dr, Aventura 1-800-327-7028* • *www.turn berryisle.com* • *$$$$$*

6 Doral Golf Resort and Spa, Miami

Internationally famous for its championship golf course. In fact, there are seven golf courses, along with 15 tennis courts, water park, health club, and a famous world-class spa. ✆ *4400 NW 87th Ave, Miami* • *1-800-713-6725* • *www.doralgolf.com* • *$$$$$*

7 Boca Raton Resort and Club

The original buildings were built by one of Florida's early visionaries, Addison Mizner, in 1926. The mix of Mediterranean styles has been carried through, and opulent, fabled luxury is everywhere, down to the marble bathrooms with original polished brass fittings. ✆ *501 East Camino Real, Boca Raton* • *1-888-491-2121* • *www. bocaresort.com* • *$$$$*

8 Cheeca Lodge, Islamorada

An amazing tropical island world unto itself, with a wonderful beach, various pools, golf, tennis, nature walks, hot-tubbing, sport fishing, snorkeling, windsurfing, etc. ✆ *Mile Marker 82, Islamorada* • *1-800-223-7637* • *www. cheeca.com* • *$$*

9 Hawk's Cay Resort, Duck Key

Exclusive Keys resort offering dolphin encounters, fishing, an offshore sailing school, scuba diving, snorkeling, parasailing, kayaking, waterskiing, glass-bottom boat tours, and so on. ✆ *Mile Marker 61* • *1-800-443-6393* • *www.hawkscay.com* • *$$$*

10 Wyndham Casa Marina Resort, Key West

Key West's first grand hotel still proudly shows its posh roots. There's a spirit of reverie contrasting with the rest of the hectic, fun-loving island. Opulent public areas lead to understated rooms, many with water views. ✆ *1500 Reynolds St, Key West* • *1-800-626-0777* • *www.casamarinakeywest. com* • *$$$$*

Note: *Unless otherwise stated, all hotels accept credit cards, have disabled access, private bathrooms, and air conditioning*

Shelborne Resort

Price Categories

For a standard, double room per night (with breakfast if included), taxes, and extra charges.

$	under $100
$$	$100–$200
$$$	$200–$250
$$$$	$250–$300
$$$$$	over $300

Surfside Retreats

1 Shelborne Resort, South Beach

Directly on the Atlantic in the heart of South Beach, this Art Deco high-rise hotel is newly restored and once again quite elegant, its surprising affordability notwithstanding. The best feature is the stylish pool. ✆ 1801 Collins Ave • 1-800-327-8757 • $$

2 Hotel Ocean, South Beach

The French-run hotel manages to blend the many worlds of Ocean Drive – the beach scene, epicurean dining scene, and the trendy club scene – with a quiet night's rest. There's a beautiful tropical courtyard, Spanish-style arched doorways, and Art Deco accent pieces. Rooms are large, well-equipped, and comfortable. ✆ 1230-38 Ocean Dr • 1-800-783-1725 • www. hotelocean.com • $$$

3 Betsy Ross Hotel, South Beach

The colonial-style hotel may seem incongruous on South Beach, but it was actually built at the same time as its Deco siblings: it just took a different fantasy turn. ✆ 1440 Ocean Drive • 1-800-755-4601 • www. betsyross hotel.com • $$

4 Ocean Surf Hotel, Miami Beach

Well north of South Beach, this appealing 1940 Nautical-Deco boutique hotel is right on the ocean. Restored in 1997, the serviceably decorated rooms offer mini-fridges, safes, and cable TV. Continental breakfast is included. ✆ 7436 Ocean Terrace • 1-800-555-0411 • www.ocean surf.com • $

5 Lago Mar, Fort Lauderdale

Lush tropical luxury right on its own flawless beach, with two pools, tennis courts, shuffleboard, and a complete spa. Rooms are very large, most with great views. Superb restaurants feature exceptional Italian cuisine at Acquario and Black Angus steaks at Chops. Very popular with families – book well in advance. ✆ 1700 S. Ocean Lane • 1-800-524-6627 • $$$

6 Windjammer Resort and Beach Club, Lauderdale-by-the-Sea

Two buildings with multi-level walkways and decks and two heated pools, plus garden areas, all combine to give this place that special resort feel. Every unit is a complete apartment in itself. ✆ 4244 El Mar Drive • 1-800-356-1220 • www.windjammerbeach resort.com • $$

7 Kona Kai Resort, Key Largo

This is a truly magical hideaway, with lovely gardens. Each guestroom is uniquely decorated in refreshing Island style, using tropical fabrics, original art, and elegant simplicity. Private beach, pool, and Jacuzzi. ✆ 97802 Overseas Hwy • 1-800-365-7829 • www. konakairesort.com • $$

8 Casa Grande, Big Pine Key

A Mediterranean-style, adults-only B&B perfectly situated on a sandy beach. The décor features high, open-beam ceilings, screened porches, rich carpets, and lazy ceiling fans. ✆ Mile Marker 33, 1619 Long Beach Drive • 305-872-2878 • $$

9 Old Town Resorts, Key West

A marvelous collection of properties including the Southernmost Hotel, Southernmost on the Beach, La Mer House, and Dewey House. Each has its own character, but all have the charm to create oases of serenity within this island's high-pitched energy. ✆ 1319 Duval Street, Key West • 1-800-934-6199 • $$

10 Grand Key Resort, Key West

The perfect place for families, or for those who want to have the choice – to party or not to party. Very close to excellent Smathers Beach. All in all, very nice facilities. ✆ 3990 S. Roosevelt Blvd, Key West • 1-888-310-1540 • $$$$

Left **Brigham Gardens Guesthouse** Center **Hotel Place St. Michel** Right **Eighteenth Street Inn**

TOP 10 Guesthouse Charmers

1 Brigham Gardens Guesthouse, SoBe

A true find in sometimes overdone SoBe. Very laid back and super-friendly, the place feels more like it's in the islands somewhere remote, yet you're just a block away from the beach intensity. The rooms have great character, and there's a tranquil garden to relax in. Book well in advance. ✆ *1411 Collins Ave • 305-531-1331 • www.brighamgardens. com • $*

2 Hotel Leon, SoBe

Unpretentious, understated, and above all comfortable, this period hotel (1929) has been tastefully, and warmly, refurbished and is a cozy hideaway with a European air. ✆ *841 Collins Ave• 305-673-3767 • www.hotelleon.com • $$*

3 Villa Paradiso Guesthouse, SoBe

All rooms have French doors that open onto the sunny courtyard and garden, and are nicely renovated and decorated with appealingly upholstered wrought iron furniture. Each accommodation has a full kitchen. ✆ *1415 Collins Ave • 305-532-0616 • www.villaparadiso hotel.com • $*

4 Hotel Place St. Michel, Coral Gables

A European-style inn built in 1926, during the Merrick heyday *(see p19).*

Each room has its own unique personality, accented by carefully chosen antiques. ✆ *162 Alcazar Ave at Ponce de Leon Blvd • 1-800-848-4683 • www.hotelplacestmichel. com • $$*

5 Eighteenth St Inn, Fort Lauderdale

Close the gate behind you and enter your own private oasis. Luxuriant vegetation and subdued lighting create a cozy, inviting atmosphere of genteel refinement and repose. Robbie's complimentary breakfasts are always gourmet-memorable. ✆ *712 SE, 18th St • 1-888-828-4466 • www. eighteenthstinn.com • $$*

6 A Little Inn by the Sea, Lauderdale-by-the-Sea

Excellent value and loaded with charm, with its leafy courtyards and splashing fountains, right on the beach. Extras include free parking, bicycle use, chaises longues, tennis, barbecue, and a heated pool. ✆ *4546 El Mar Drive • 1-800-492-0311 • www.alittleinn.com • $$*

7 Barnacle Bed & Breakfast, Big Pine Key

Tucked among towering palm trees on a white sandy beach, this is an intriguing Caribbean-style home where leisurely breezes prevail. Unique furnishings in each room. Breakfast is served in the

atrium overlooking the ocean. ✆ *1557 Long Beach Drive • 1-800-465-9100 • $$*

8 The Gardens Hotel, Key West

In a serene, shaded world of botanical gardens, this plantation-style property is certainly Key West's grande dame among guesthouses. Five buildings comprise the hotel, including a Bahamian "eyebrow" cottage. All rooms have garden views and most have Jacuzzis. All in all, sumptuous. ✆ *526 Angela St • 1-800-526-2664 • www.gardenshotel. com • $$$$*

9 Marquesa Hotel, Key West

Built in 1884, the extravagant compound of four exquisitely restored "conch" houses is now set amid lush greenery. All rooms and suites have marble bathrooms. ✆ *600 Fleming St • 1-800-869-4631 • www.marquesa. com • $$$$*

10 The Mermaid & the Alligator, Key West

One of Key West's very finest, a 1904 beauty, with colonial Caribbean décor and wonderful gardens. Rooms have period furnishings, and they feel private and deeply cozy. Full breakfast is served by the pool; wine in the afternoons. ✆ *729 Truman Ave • 1-800-773-1894 • www.kwmer maid.com • $$*

Note: *Unless otherwise stated, all hotels accept credit cards, have disabled access, private bathrooms, and air conditioning*

Southwinds Motel

Price Categories	
For a standard, double room per night (with breakfast if included), taxes, and extra charges.	**$** under $100
	$$ $100–$200
	$$$ $200–$250
	$$$$ $250–$300
	$$$$$ over $300

🔟 Exceptional Value Places

1 Astor Place, SoBe
Stay just a couple of blocks away from the beach and get a top-quality 1936 Deco gem for much less outlay. Rooms are large and fully soundproofed, bathrooms have marble walls and floors, and the pool area has gardenia hedges and night-blooming jasmine. ✪ *956 Washington Ave • 1-800-270-4981 • $$*

2 Cadet Hotel, SoBe
With its festive Deco façade wrapped around a corner, this little find has one of the most enviable locations in South Beach. Comfortable, rather stylish rooms, and very efficient and professional service. Clark Gable once stayed here. ✪ *1701 James Ave • www.cadethotel.com • 1-800-432-2338 • $$*

3 James Hotel, SoBe
From the moment you cross the threshold, everywhere you look there are brightly painted tiles, murals, and all manner of whimsical touches, including at least five different "Welcome" signs. Make reservations well in advance – the location is unbeatable. ✪ *1680 James Ave • 305-531-1125 • $*

4 Tide Vacation Apartments, Hollywood Beach
Facing the sea, directly on Hollywood Beach's Broadwalk, each accommodation is a spacious efficiency (self-catering) apartment. ✪ *2800 North Surf Rd, at Coolidge • 954-923-3864 • www.tide apartments.com • Limited dis acc • $$*

5 Best Western Beachcomber, Pompano Beach
An extraordinarily exclusive feel at very reasonable prices. Accommodations range from villas, to rooms with or without kitchens, to penthouse suites. The distinctive wrap-around balconies add an unusually plush touch to the architecture. ✪ *1200 S. Ocean Blvd • 1-866-568-7025 • $$*

6 Kon Tiki Resort, Islamorada
The homey Olde Keys experience at its best. Not at all stylish, in fact, just a little bit raw, but very welcoming and comfortable. It has gardens, a heated freshwater pool, a sandy beach, and protected lagoon on Florida Bay, and a boat ramp. ✪ *81200 Overseas Hwy., Mile Marker 82 • 305-664-4702 • www.theflorida keys.com/kontiki • $$*

7 Duval House, Key West
These gracious Victorian twins and their white picket fence will win your heart. The rooms are accented with lots of wicker and florals, and everyone seems extraordinarily friendly. The location is unsurpassed for convenience. ✪ *815 Duval St • 1-800-223-8825 • www.duvalhousekeywest. com • $$*

8 Atlantic Shores Resort, Key West
Key West's only ocean-front adult alternative resort, catering to the most mixed clientele you can imagine. The biggest draw is the clothing-optional pool and sundeck right out on the Atlantic, which is pretty much "Party Central" most hours of the day and night. ✪ *511 South St • 1-800-598-6988 • www. atlanticshoresresort.com • Limited dis acc • $$*

9 Abaco Inn, Key West
On a secluded lane in the lush heart of the Old Town district, not far from amenities. All rooms are smoke-free and decorated in cool, restful colors. Out back, there's a relaxing tropical garden. ✪ *415 Julia St • 1-800-358-6307 • www.abaco-inn.com • $$*

10 Southwind Motel, Key West
An old-fashioned, unpretentious motel. There's a large fresh-water pool and sundeck, set in a tropical garden. Some rooms have kitchenettes, and all guests have off-street parking. ✪ *1321 Simonton St • 305-296-2215 • www.keywest southwind.com • $$*

Left **Clay Hotel and Youth Hostel** Right **Peter Miller Hotel**

 Hostels and Budget

1 Clay Hotel and Youth Hostel, SoBe

This enchanting Spanish-style place, built in 1925 and beautifully refurbished, also happens to be the biggest bargain in the Western World and is always teeming with international youth. Book very far in advance to get a place. ⌖ *1438 Washington Avenue, South Beach • 1-800-379-2529 • www.clayhotel.com • $*

2 Banana Bungalow, Miami Beach

Very '50s motel Moderne, this is a busy and youthful establishment that's always got a crowd around the pool. Rooms tend to be stark but adequate. The only drawback is that it's not in the heart of South Beach. ⌖ *2360 Collins Ave, Miami Beach • 1-800-746-7835 • www.banana bungalow.com • $*

3 Miami Beach Travelers' Hostel

One of the cheapest places right in the middle of the SoBe action, this hostel radiates a fun-loving atmosphere of camaraderie, even though it is a bit grotty. Amenities include Internet access, kitchen, and laundry. ⌖ *236 9th St, South Beach • 1-800-978-6787 • www.sobehostel.com • $*

4 Tropics Hotel and Hostel, SoBe

This is a genuine Art Deco building, complete with neon marquee, in one of the most desirable locations on South Beach. It's clean and comfortable and, given the location, worth two to three times the asking price. There's even a pool. Book far in advance. ⌖ *1550 Collins Ave, South Beach • 305-531-0361 • www.tropicshotel.com • $*

5 Peter Miller Hotel, SoBe

Authentic 1935 Deco, although a bit down-at-the-heel, this place promotes itself as "the best deal on South Beach" – the rates are extremely good if you negotiate for a week or so. Rooms are large and comfortable. Tends toward an older clientele. ⌖ *1900 Collins Ave, South Beach • 305-531-7611 • $*

6 Berkeley Shore Hotel, SoBe

Definitely one of the coolest Deco buildings around, with its elaborate façade, and riot of Island-style color inside. The proprietors and staff are mostly Cubans – there's a vivacity about the place that feels Caribbean. Rooms are spacious, though basic. Many have kitchenettes. ⌖ *1610 Collins Ave, South Beach • 305-531-5731 • $*

7 Green Island Inn, Fort Lauderdale

An amazing deal. The whole ambience is so inviting and spacious it feels like a resort. Homey touches are everywhere, and each room has its own uniquely tropical look, as well as a full kitchen. Book well in advance. ⌖ *3300 NE 27th St, Fort Lauderdale Beach • 954-566-8951 • www.green islandinn.com • $*

8 Florida Beach Hostel, Fort Lauderdale

A clean and fresh place near the beach, with a nice rooftop patio and tropical garden courtyard for picnicking. There's free parking and some free food, too. ⌖ *2115 N. Ocean Blvd, Fort Lauderdale • 954-567-7275 • www. fortlauderdalehostel.com • $*

9 Budget Key West

No pool, no lobby, no frills, but it's clean, comfortable, bright, secure, within easy walking distance of most places in Old Town, and the vernacular architecture is appealing. All rooms have a kitchenette. ⌖ *1031 Eaton St, Key West • 1-800-403-2866 • www.budget keywest.com • $$*

10 Key West Youth Hostel

Offers snorkeling trips and scuba instruction, plus bike rentals. It has a courtyard, picnic area, and game rooms, but only 10 private rooms, so book well in advance. ⌖ *718 South St, Key West • 305-296-5719 • www. keywesthostel.com • $*

Note: *Unless otherwise stated, all hotels accept credit cards, have disabled access, private bathrooms, and air conditioning*

Price Categories	
For a standard, double room per night (with breakfast if included), taxes, and extra charges.	$ under $100
	$$ $100–$200
	$$$ $200–$250
	$$$$ $250–$300
	$$$$$ over $300

Royal Palms Resort

TOP 10 Gay and Lesbian Hotels

1 Island House, South Beach and Haulover Beach

Two properties for gay males, with a wide variety of room configurations available in both places, all at very reasonable rates. ◎ 1428 Collins Ave, South Beach / 715 82nd St at Harding Ave, Surfside, Haulover Beach • 1-800-382-2422 for both • www.islandhousesouthbeach.com • Some rooms have shared bathroom facilities • $

2 Jefferson House, SoBe

In a quiet neighborhood, five blocks from the beach, is one of the best gay and lesbian guesthouses in Miami. Attractions include a sun deck, pool, wine-and-cheese parties, and a gourmet breakfast by the pool. Primarily gay men. ◎ 1018 Jefferson Ave at 10th St, South Beach • 1-877-599-5247 • www.jeffersonhouse.com • $$

3 South Beach Villas

Away from the main SoBe action, this is the place to come if you want seclusion and tranquility. The setting is lush, there's a heated pool, Jacuzzi, large sundeck, and cable TV and sound system in every room. Primarily gay men. ◎ 1201 West Ave at 12th St, South Beach • 1-888-429-7623 • www.sobevillas.com • $$

4 Pineapple Point, Fort Lauderdale

Fort Lauderdale's premier accommodation for gay men is like a tropical rain forest, complete with orchids and a clothing-optional pool. Every comfort has been seen to in the rooms. ◎ 315 NE 16 Terrace, Fort Lauderdale • 1-888-844-7295 • www.pineapplepoint.com • $

5 The Flamingo, Fort Lauderdale

A thoroughly pleasant place for gay men only, just two blocks from the beach. The interior exudes an understated colonial charm, with soothing fountains, manicured gardens, a clothing-optional pool, four-poster beds, and white-on-white bedding. ◎ 2727 Terramar St, Fort Lauderdale • 1-800-283-4786 • www.theflamingoresort.com • $$

6 Royal Palms Resort, Fort Lauderdale

Gay men only are catered to here, in a lush tropical setting with clothing-optional pool. Rooms and suites have two-line phones, CD-players, high-speed internet access. ◎ 2901 Terramar, Fort Lauderdale Beach • 1-800-237-7256 • www.royalpalms.com • $$$

7 Island House for Men, Key West

For gay men only, this beautiful property is clothing-optional and very cruisy, featuring a poolside café, sauna and steam room, bar, gym, and erotic video lounge.

◎ 1129 Fleming St, Key West • 1-800-890-6284 • www.islandhousekeywest.com • $$

8 Coral Tree Inn and Oasis Guesthouse, Key West

The award-winning male-only duo, on opposite sides of Fleming St, form the largest accommodation option on a very gay block. All properties along here are beautifully restored period buildings with heated pools, Jacuzzis, and all the charms for which Key West is famous. ◎ 822 & 823 Fleming St, Key West • 1-800-362-7477 • www.keywest-allmale.com • $$

9 Lighthouse Court Guesthouse Resort, Key West

Another clothing-optional, gay-males-only, "happening" resort comprising 10 restored houses a block off Duval Street. ◎ 902 Whitehead St, Key West • 305-294-9588 • www.lighthousecourt.com • $$

10 Pearl's Rainbow, Key West

Key West's only women-only guesthouse, well located just two blocks from the beach. You'll find extensive shady and sunny decks, two pools, two hot tubs, and Pearl's Patio, a poolside bar. Continental breakfast is included in the price. ◎ 525 United St, Key West • 1-800-749-6696 • www.pearlsrainbow.com • $$

Index

Page numbers in **bold** type refer to main entries

Acknowledgements

The Author

Jeffrey Kennedy is a freelance travel writer who divides his time between the Iberian Peninsula and the USA.

Produced by
BLUE ISLAND PUBLISHING
Editorial Director Rosalyn Thiro
Art Director Stephen Bere
Associate Editor Michael Ellis
Designer Lee Redmond
Picture Research Ellen Root
Research Assistance Amaia Allende
Proofread, Fact-check & Index Mary Sutherland

Main Photographer Peter Wilson
Additional Photography Max Alexander, Dave King, Neil Mersh, Paolo Pulga, Clive Streeter, Stephen Whitehorn, Linda Whitwam

Cartography Encompass Graphics

AT DORLING KINDERSLEY
Series Publisher Douglas Amrine
Publishing Managers Fay Franklin, Jane Ewart
Senior Art Editor Marisa Renzullo
Cartographic Editor Caspar Morris
DTP Jason Little, Conrad van Dyk
Production Melanie Dowland

Picture Credits

Placement Key: t–top; tl–top left; tr–top right; tc–top center; tcl–top center left; c–center; cr–center right; b–bottom; bl–bottom left; br–bottom right.

AFP: 49br;

CARNAVAL MIAMI: 40b; COCONUT GROVE ARTS FESTIVAL: 40tl; CORBIS: 39cr; Tony Arruza 112-3; Bettmann 39tr; Mitchell Gerber 39br, 49tr;

EVERGLADES NATIONAL PARK: 119tl;

FLORIDA GRAND OPERA: Photo Debra Hesser 38tr; Tom J Franks: 40c;

BARBARA GILLMAN GALLERY: 43br; GREATER MIAMI CONVENTION AND VISITORS BUREAU: 8–9, 14–15, 28t, 35l all, 38c, 64-5, 66c, 70tcl, 72t, 74tl, 74tr, 115b, 136tl;

HISPANIC HERITAGE FESTIVAL: 41bl; HISTORICAL MUSEUM OF SOUTHERN FLORIDA: 42tr;

INTERNATIONAL MANGO FESTIVAL: Suzanne Kores 40tr; ITALIAN RENAISSANCE FESTIVAL: Bill Sims 41tl;

LINCOLN THEATER: 38tc; LOWE ART MUSEUM, UNIVERSITY OF MIAMI: 20t/20b/21 all, 21b (c) Duane Hanson/ VAGA, New York and DACS, London 2002, 42tl;

MIAMI-DADE COUNTY FAIR AND EXPOSITION: 40tc; MORIKAMI MUSEUM FLORIDA: 36tr;

NHPA: Trevor McDonald 32b; Tom & Therisa Stack 33t; STUART NEWMAN ASSOCIATES: 121tr; NORTON MUSEUM OF ART: 42br;

PALM BEACH COUNTY CONVENTION AND VISITORS BUREAU: 32T; PICTURES COLOUR LIBRARY: 128b, 129b; SOUTH BEACH GAY MEN'S CHORUS: Roberto Ferreira 38tl; THE EIGHTEENTH STREET INN: Michael Murphy Photography 150tr; THEATER OF THE SEA: 116tr;

WOLFSONIAN-FLORIDA INTERNATIONAL UNIVERSITY: 7tr, 22r, 22b, 22l, 23c, 23b, 23t, 42tc, 42c.

All other images are © Dorling Kindersley. For more information see www.dkimages.com

Cartography Credits

Martin Darlison (Encompass Graphics Ltd)

DK publishes a wide range of guidebooks, including nearly 20 in this Eyewitness Top Ten series and more than 70 in the award-winning Eyewitness Travel Guide series. To see our complete range of guides, phrasebooks and maps, visit us at
www.dk.com